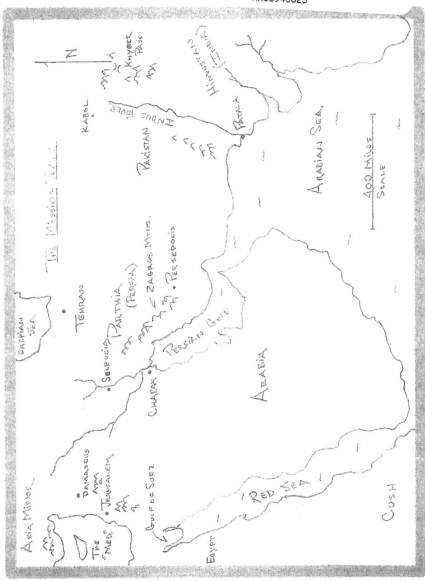

The Mission Area

N

KHYBER PASS

HINDUSTAN

KABOL

INDUS RIVER

PAKISTAN

PATALA

ARABIAN SEA

400 MILES
SCALE

CASPIAN SEA

TEHRAN

SELEUCIA (PARTHIA)
(PERSIA)
ZAGROS MTNS.
PERSEPOLIS

PERSIAN GULF

CHARAX

ARABIA

ASIA MINOR

DAMASCUS
JERUSALEM
THE "MED."
GULF OF SUEZ

RED SEA

EGYPT

CUSH

"Worn Sandals"

The Missing Years of Jesus

"Worn Sandals"

The Missing Years of Jesus

Jennifer Taylor Wojcik
Philip G. Lilly D.Min.

ISBN-13: 9781978205512
ISBN-10: 1978205511
Library of Congress Control Number: 2017917246
CreateSpace Independent Publishing Platform
North Charleston, South Carolina

Table of Contents

Prologue

Worn Sandals is not a flawless work of historic fact, nor is it all historical fiction. Rather, it is a blend of both.

This is the story of Jesus of Nazareth; the paths He chose, the distances He traveled to learn, teach, and heal, and the sheer magnitude that this fully God/ fully man experienced during His earthly life. In addition to a walk through the life of Christ, *Worn Sandals* shares what could have happened during those missing years: specifically birth to age twelve—and from age twelve to thirty.

Those "missing" years aren't addressed in the Bible, but history reflects the state of the world during that time. Customs, laws that were enacted, education, health issues, and governmental influence are recorded in history, and in this world, Jesus lived and grew from a child to an adult.

No doubt, Jesus stubbed His toe, took a tumble playing with friends, and was tempted by everyday challenges. He was likely loved as well as rebuked, accepted as well as rejected, and brought up as a typical Jewish boy. That traditional Jewish upbringing centered on an education of the Law and learning the trade of his father. And while Mary and Joseph knew He was special, they most likely did not convey that to Him or treat Him differently from the other children.

After His bar mitzvah, Jesus was probably selected by more than one Jewish family as the prospective husband for their daughters but chose friendships rather than marital relationship. He likely traveled, meeting with elders and teachers while absorbing all the world's information at His disposal before beginning His ministerial life.

Jennifer Taylor Wojcik
Philip G. Lilly D.Min.

Worn Sandals follows the chronology of Jesus's life. By way of biblical history and paying homage to historically recorded events of the time, we have compiled scenes that could have happened to Him and to those around Him. We have added scripture passages where appropriate and hope you find them helpful in setting the stage for the exploration of Jesus's life and travels. And having read more about Him, we hope you will feel as though you have figuratively walked in His shoes—His *worn sandals.*

At the appointed time, Jesus came "into His own"—He taught, preached, healed, and conveyed His message of salvation. Jesus lived life as a man and knew life as God.

> *But you, Bethlehem Ephrathah, though you are small among the clans of Judah, out of you will come for me one who will be ruler over Israel, whose origins are from of old, from ancient times (*Micah 5:2 NIV*).*

We hope you enjoy the journey.

When I sent you without purse, bag or sandals, did you lack anything? **(Luke 22:35 NIV)**

Introduction:
Jesus of Nazareth

He was known as simply Jesus, son of the carpenter Joseph and his wife, Mary. To the average person, he was just a kid—smart and curious, but still just a kid.

He grew up in a typical Jewish household with no special treatment or conditions. While he was the firstborn to Joseph and Mary, passing years produced siblings who looked to him as simply their big brother.

While his parents knew he was special, it was important to them that Jesus was allowed to be a typical well-mannered, well-taught boy who would grow into the best man he could be. They believed that when the time was right, he would *know* exactly who he was.

It was the time in history when families tended to live in close proximity to one another, often sharing a home or living in a "complex" of sorts, in order to share the duties and responsibilities of family. Living in shared quarters gave the group the ability to allocate chores like cooking, washing clothes, and child-rearing. It also meant that families were closely knit and never short of companionship regardless of the age ranges that made up the group.

Youngsters had built-in role models and family members from which to learn. Grandparents were cherished and seen as well-versed senior members of the clan. They were also honored and revered for living to a ripe old age—woefully short by modern-day standards, typically around forty years old.

That also meant that when a young person *came of age*, she or he was barely past ten or eleven. Marriages often occurred at roughly twelve years of age and were arranged or selected and then negotiated across families.

The Jewish people followed the Law (of Moses) and were expected to do so. Tradition required that a baby boy be brought to the temple or synagogue eight days after birth to be circumcised. At the same time, the boy's name would be entered in "the book"—the official recording of male births. The child would be "presented" to God—thereby committing his life to God's service and making him one of God's own.

Jewish children were nurtured and primarily cared for by their mothers (and extended family members) until they became school age—roughly six or seven years old. They would then attend school at the local synagogue and be taught more about the Law, Jewish traditions, and the Jewish way of life.

Jewish boys were charged with learning the trade of their fathers—to perpetuate the family's economic standing and to assure that their heritage was respected. Jewish girls were taught by female family members and contributed to the more domestic side of life—learning to be in charge of hearth and home. They were also responsible to know the Law and charged to abide by its doctrines.

Most of us are familiar with the story of Jesus's birth. It was neither ordinary nor common, and worth revisiting. First—meet Elizabeth and her husband, Zechariah, so that you will understand the family connections to Jesus and see God's plan in retrospect. (Hindsight is often, if not always, twenty-twenty.)

I

Elizabeth and Mary

A priest named Zechariah and his wife, Elizabeth, lived under the rule of King Herod of Judea. Both Zechariah and Elizabeth were well along in years and both were believed to be righteous in the sight of God. Though they observed the Lord's commands blamelessly, they remained childless due to Elizabeth's inability to conceive a child. In that day and age, this was considered a disgrace among the people of Judea.

Being well respected and revered by his peers, Zechariah was chosen to go into the temple of the Lord to burn incense.

As Zechariah approached the temple, an angel of the Lord appeared to him. The angel identified himself as Gabriel and said he had been sent by God to deliver great news. Naturally, Zechariah was stricken with fear, but the angel told him not to be afraid, that his prayers about a child had been heard by God and that Elizabeth would bear him a son.

Finding this news mind-boggling, Zechariah asked the angel how he could be sure of this news. Because Zechariah doubted, Gabriel told him he would be unable to speak until the day the prophecy was fulfilled.

As Zechariah left the temple, he was indeed unable to speak to the people waiting for him. With his duties of burning incense done, Zechariah returned home mute—unable to share the news he had received from the angel.

Just as Gabriel had said, Elizabeth became pregnant and remained in seclusion for five months. Although Elizabeth was delighted that her prayers had been answered and she was finally with child, she had moments of skepticism and concern.

Elizabeth knew in her heart this child was destined to be a leader; one who would guide his people in the ways of the Lord, and she did everything in her power to protect the child. She prayed daily for his safety.

☙❧

When Elizabeth was in her sixth month of pregnancy, God sent the angel Gabriel to a virgin named Mary of Nazareth in Galilee. Mary and Elizabeth were first cousins.

Gabriel assured Mary she should not be afraid. He told her she had been chosen to give birth to the Son of God and that God would give this child the throne of David. Gabriel instructed Mary that the child's name would be Jesus, and that he would rule over Jacob's descendants forever.

When Mary asked how a virgin could give birth, Gabriel explained that God's Holy Spirit would overshadow her and she would conceive the child as a result. Gabriel also told Mary that her cousin Elizabeth was pregnant and was now in her sixth month of pregnancy.

Shocked and surprised but believing the angel, Mary told Gabriel that she was God's willing servant and that she would fulfill His chosen destiny in her life.

> *God sent Gabriel...to a virgin pledged to be married to a man named Joseph, a descendant of David. The virgin's name was Mary...Do not be afraid Mary; you have found favor with God. You will conceive and give birth to a son and you are to call him Jesus...The Holy Spirit will come on you, and the power of the Most High will overshadow you. The holy one to be born will be called the Son of God* (Luke 1:27 NIV).

☙❧

After the angel Gabriel left Mary, she immediately prepared to visit Elizabeth. Hurriedly, Mary went to Judea and entered the home of Zechariah.

When Mary arrived and called out to Elizabeth, the baby Elizabeth was carrying literally leapt in her womb. At the sight of Mary, Elizabeth said, "Blessed are you among women, and blessed is the child you will bear" (Luke 1:42 NIV).

Mary spent the next three months with Elizabeth, leaving just prior to the birth of her son, John, who would later be known as John the Baptist.

During those three months, the two cousins discussed both their thoughts and fears about their pregnancies. Neither of them had firsthand knowledge of what to expect or what to do. They shared their gratitude to God for His blessings but naturally expressed their concerns about the circumstances they were in.

Here was Elizabeth—elderly, and well beyond normal child-bearing years—pregnant for the first time. By now, she had concealed herself from the residents of Judea, who would surely make disparaging comments about her "condition" at this stage in her life. It was a catch-twenty-two situation for her. While "the curse" of being a barren woman had been eliminated, Elizabeth was privately concerned about her ability to carry a child to full term.

During their talks together, Mary and Elizabeth realized they shared many of the same fears. Neither had previous experience to rely on or a way to relate to their ever-changing bodies. And while each woman's fears were for different reasons, both had been propelled into uncharted waters.

Being a virgin, young and recently betrothed, Mary feared that Joseph would now either reject her by believing she had been with another man or marry her only to give her child a family name and then divorce her.

One can just imagine the *humanness* Mary was feeling. While honored to be chosen by the Lord to bring His son into the world, Mary's responsibilities in delivering and then raising this child were unimaginable.

Being related to Elizabeth served Mary well, in that she had a confidante, a mentor, and because of their age difference, a mother-figure. Spending these formative months in the presence of her cousin who was also giving birth to a "miracle baby" surely had to be a source of comfort for young Mary.

Having so much, yet knowing so little, the two relied on their faith as well as their heritage. Both women had been chosen by God, and an intricate plan had been woven to enhance the lives of their offspring by one another and to one another.

Because God's messages were delivered by the angel Gabriel, the women were comforted. Each of them knew her child was being placed in the world for a divine purpose. And, having been told so by the angel, they knew Elizabeth's son would prepare the way for Jesus and that Jesus would rule the world as the son of God. Both Elizabeth and Mary recognized they were part of something much larger than they knew or could understand.

Often, one cannot readily see God's plans as they are unfolding, yet in hindsight they appear clear and divine.

II

Long Road to the House of Bread

So Joseph also went up from the town of Nazareth in Galilee to Judea, to Bethlehem the town of David, because he belonged to the house and line of David. He went there to register with Mary, who was pledged to be married to him and was expecting a child (Luke 2:4–5 NIV).

The arrival in Bethlehem marked the end of an arduous journey for Joseph and his new wife, Mary, who was expecting her first child. It was late, and there was a distinct chill in the evening air.

Joseph and Mary had been looking for a place where they could rest and get food. Although there were several village guesthouses in Bethlehem, they were filled with those who had arrived earlier. Like Joseph and Mary, their purpose in traveling to Bethlehem was to be counted in the census, mandated by Emperor Augustus.

Joseph and Mary wandered the barren streets of the city for hours before they came upon a nondescript inn. It was late in the evening, and most places were closed for the night. The inn they were approaching was like most of the guesthouses in the city: modest with a flat roof and a partially underground area that housed the owner's animals.

Mary, being more than weary of travel, begged Joseph to just check with the innkeeper and see if there was *any* place they could stay.

After rapping on the door and getting no answer, Joseph looked at his wife, who was to deliver her baby at any time, and shook his head. His love and concern for her outweighed any embarrassment he might have had, so he knocked again, more enthusiastically this time.

Jennifer Taylor Wojcik
Philip G. Lilly D.Min.

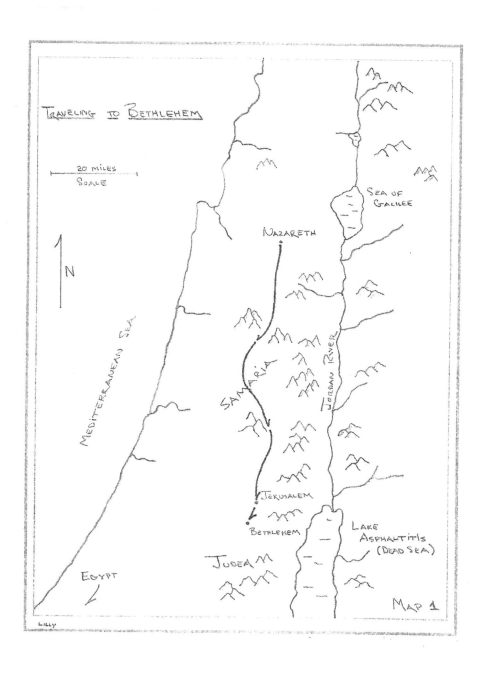

The innkeeper, who had obviously been awakened from sleep, opened the door only slightly and abruptly said, "We have no room," and started to close the door. Joseph stopped the door closing by placing his walking stick inside to jam it.

Joseph pleaded, "Sir, you need to understand that we will take any safe place you might have." Motioning toward Mary, he said, "She is pregnant, and we have looked everywhere in town. She cannot continue on tonight. If you would just please reconsider and allow us to spend the night, we will try to find other lodging tomorrow."

Peering from behind the innkeeper, a woman suddenly appeared. She too had been awakened from sleep.

"Look, we have one area and one only, but that's in the stable where the animals are. If you will take that, then we can all get some rest. Where is your wife?" asked the woman.

As Joseph stepped aside, the woman saw Mary sitting astride their donkey.

"My goodness!" she exclaimed. "She looks like she could give birth at any minute." And turning to the innkeeper, she said, "We have to help this poor girl. She's probably starving too." She looked back at Joseph. "Have you two had anything to eat today?"

"Not for hours, ma'am," replied Joseph. "We thought we should find a place to rest first, but we've been unsuccessful. Please, if you will allow us to stay in your stable, we would be most grateful."

She pushed past the innkeeper and said, "Follow me," making her way to Mary and the donkey. She whispered to Mary, "It will be fine; you can stay with us. I'll make sure you are safe and comfortable."

Mary nodded and thanked the woman as she was being led to the stable area.

As the woman was settling the couple into the barn, she asked Mary, "Have you two been following the large star?"

Mary wasn't sure what she meant. She answered simply, "We've been on this journey to satisfy the ruling to be here for the census, but perhaps Joseph knows of the star. I don't know how he knew where to go in the darkness."

"*This* star," said the woman as she opened the wooden window, pointing outside. "Everyone is talking about it and wondering what it means."

Mary observed the bright star with a sense of wonderment. "It is indeed a heavenly sight and no doubt helped Joseph find our refuge here with you. Thank you so much for your kindness."

"I'm happy to help. Is this your first child?"

Mary gently nodded her head.

"As soon as I get you settled and comfortable, I'll find something for you and your husband to eat…" the woman said.

"He is *newly* my husband," said Mary, in a sweet, small voice. Gazing at the woman, Mary expected a negative reaction but did not get one.

"I'm not going to judge you," said the woman as she tucked more straw around Mary. "The innkeeper isn't my husband, at least not technically. My husband died a while back, and the innkeeper is his brother. By law, he's supposed to marry me and take care of me, but our circumstances are complicated. So don't you worry. There will be no judgment passed on you here. By the way, what is your name?"

"I am Mary, and my husband's name is Joseph. And what is your name?" Mary asked.

"I am Rachael, and Nathan is the innkeeper. Now, Mary, you rest, and I will return with food for you and Joseph."

When Rachael returned, she brought bread, cheese, and dates for the couple to share. While they ate, Nathan tended to the donkey and the other animals.

Nathan, now being more accommodating, said, "Sorry to put you in here with all the livestock, but it's the best we can do. Maybe we'll have better luck finding you something nicer tomorrow."

"We are fine here, sir, and appreciate your kindness. And I notice there are some boards in need of replacement. I am a carpenter by trade and will be happy to do work here in exchange for your hospitality," said Joseph.

"That would be fine, young man, but tonight you should relax and rest. I'll just close this window to keep out the chill," Nathan said as he moved toward the wooden hatch.

Mary said, "Sir, would you mind leaving that slightly open? I so love looking at that bright, shining star. It is magnificent, don't you think?"

"Yes, madam, as you wish," replied Nathan as he left the wooden window slightly ajar. "People all over Bethlehem are talking about it. Word is that it doesn't happen very often—it's never happened before in my lifetime. Please sleep well. I'll check on you two in the morning."

"Shalom. Thank you," Joseph said.

As Mary drifted into sleep, she kept her eyes on the flickering star. She knew it was a sign. Mary dreamed that night of a tiny pair of sandals—sandals that only her soon-to-be-born son could fill.

Morning broke, and Mary and Joseph had slept well and were thankful to have had shelter through the night. Mary related her dream to Joseph.

"You could make him a pair of sandals, couldn't you, Joseph?"

Joseph's mind quickly leapt back to a former time in his life...

◦◦ᘓᗷᗄ◦◦

"Yosep, Yosep!" It was young Joseph's mother, Rhonda, screaming out to him. "Joseph, Joseph—you forgot to secure the gate to the goat's pen! Go there now before they escape. Your father will be very angry with you and likely whip you for leaving the gate open."

Joseph knew better. His father, Jacob, was a mild-mannered man and definitely not the disciplinarian his mother made him out to be. But best to hustle back over to the gate and secure it properly. In his rush to catch up with some friends, he had tied a sloppy knot around the gatepost, and it had probably come undone. The family goats would surely be on the loose with an open gate. Joseph quickly secured the gate with a tight knot. Now he was done!

As Joseph turned to walk away from the pen, a protruding nail at the bottom of the gate caught the leather strap on his left sandal. As he moved away, it immediately snapped his sandal strap in half, and the sandal spun around the bottom of his foot, falling to the ground. "Oh no!" he cried out.

His mother heard the noise from inside the house and called to him, "What's wrong, Joseph?"

He quickly responded, "Nothing, Mother; I was just yelling at the goats to get back." He knew that his mother must not know of this latest slipup.

"Good, now go on and meet those friends of yours," she responded.

Joseph put the torn sandal in his pocket and left to meet his friends. Heading down several alleys toward the village center, Joseph thought about his options for repairing his sandal. "Ouch, ouch." He winced as the pebbles under his bare foot slowed him down.

"Ah, I can stop at my father's shop," he thought. "It's right off the village square, and he can fix anything." Within minutes he was at the back entrance to his father's shop.

His father heard someone at the back doorway and turned to see Joseph limping in. "What's wrong, son?"

The seven-year-old sheepishly said, "I've torn my sandal, Father."

"Sit down on the bench, and let's take a look." The first thing Joseph's father did was clean the bruised foot, signaling to his son that everything was okay.

The young Joseph had always been fascinated with his father's craft. As he sat on the bench, his eyes wandered around the shop, looking at all the tools and implements of his father's trade.

Father Jacob was a carpenter. But he was not just an ordinary carpenter, because he was a maker of wheels. Joseph had often heard his father say, "Anyone can make a door or a table, but it takes a craftsman to make a good wheel. Good wheels make a difference in our community."

Joseph was proud of his father. Anytime he saw a cart or wagon go by, he would tell his friends, "My father made that wheel. I know that because it is a good one."

In no time Joseph's sandal was repaired.

"Son, you are ready to go," Jacob said, looking down at his son. "Are you off to see your friends now?"

Joseph responded, "Can I stay here and work with you, Father?"

"Certainly, son; I can teach you to be a wheel maker." The two smiled at one another as Joseph slipped the repaired sandal on his foot. It was time for the young man to learn his father's trade.

❧

Joseph's attention snapped back to reality when Mary again asked him, "Joseph—you could make him a pair of sandals, couldn't you?"

Joseph looked at her inquisitively, as if this dream had foretold her delivery was near. "Indeed, Mary—whatever you want for him, he will have."

Joseph exited the barn and found Rachael and her neighbors preparing fresh bread in the enclave. When Rachael saw Joseph, she stood and gave him some freshly baked bread. "Here, eat this," she said. "I will take some bread to Mary. I'd like to check on her and see if she needs anything."

Joseph thanked Rachael for the breakfast and for taking care of Mary.

Rachael had prepared a basket for the couple, including linens from her own home, and added the fresh bread and cheese before scurrying off to see Mary. When she entered the stable, she saw that Mary was clutching her stomach.

"Mary, is it time?" she asked.

Mary smiled and said, "I don't believe so, but I cannot be sure. As I told you, this is my first child, so I have no idea how I will know when the time comes."

"Don't worry, Mary. As a midwife, I have helped deliver many babies, and I am here to help you too. Believe me, when it is time for your baby to come into this world, you will know," Rachael reassured her. "But for now, let's get some nourishment in you. I brought fresh bread, cheese, and cow's milk. You eat and enjoy."

As Mary ate, Rachael moved about the stalls, working and sharing more about her life in Bethlehem.

"The name Rachael means 'female sheep,' correct?" asked Mary.

Rachael replied, "Yes, it does; my mother felt it would be a pretty and gentle name."

Mary responded, saying, "It fits you. I find you to be gentle and pretty as well."

"It's nice to have someone to talk to. People have judged me," she said to Mary, "as I'm sure they have judged you. Like most people, I was poor from birth, but I always wanted something more out of life. I've done some things I'm not proud to admit, but when I look back on them, I see that I didn't have much of a choice," Rachael said.

"So what about your late husband?" asked Mary, "That had to be a very difficult time for you. Do you have any children?"

"No, we did not have children. My husband was a hardworking man, and he made a decent living as a stonecutter. He died after getting an infection in a wound. Yes, it was hard. I am a barren woman, never blessed with children. I think that's what made me become good at helping other people give birth. Some didn't want my help once they realized that I'm a pagan, some say a heathen. You see, Mary, when you are raised to worship idols and serve many gods, people in Israel tend to look down on you."

"But if you were raised to believe in many gods, how would you know about anything else?" Mary asked. "I am Jewish, and I believe there is but one God worthy of worship, but I've been exposed to many beliefs, including those who believe there is more than one god."

"Well, I just don't think it matters that much. I try to do the right thing, but no matter what god I make sacrifices to, life just gets harder."

"What do you mean when you say that, Rachael?" asked Mary.

"Well, as I told you, my husband was a good man—and look what happened to him. Now I'm obliged to marry Nathan, and he is not a good provider. As a matter of fact, we're probably in the tightest financial place we've ever been. If we can't pay off our debts soon, we will lose everything—our inn, our livestock, all of it. There are never enough denarii to make ends meet. That's why we haven't married. If he loses everything or if he dies before we marry, I can at least try to start my life over with someone else."

"I'm reminded of a psalm," said Mary. "As I said, I believe there is only one true God. That psalm says, 'From my distress I called upon the Lord; the Lord answered me and set me in a large place. The Lord is for me; I will not fear: What can man do to me?...It is better to take refuge in the Lord than to trust in man.' (Psalm 118:5 NASB)

"So, Rachael, if you find yourself in that tight place, pray to the one God over heaven and earth and ask Him to put you in a large place. I know He will answer your prayer. He has surely answered all of mine," Mary said.

"You are a Jew, and yet you would accept kindness and friendship from the likes of me?" asked Rachael.

"What I see when I look at you is that you are a loving and kind woman. I understand that you haven't heard the good news about the one true, everlasting God and the prophets' prediction of the *Anointed One*—the Messiah who is to come. I believe that God led Joseph and me to you and your inn if for no other reason so that I could tell you about God and His greatness. As a matter of fact, Rachael, I now count you as a true friend," Mary answered.

"Then I must seriously consider what you have said, Mary. You obviously are wise beyond your years. But what does God think of you and your unborn child who was surely conceived out of wedlock?" Rachael asked.

"I will tell you, Rachael. This child was given to me by God, and it is His blessed son that I carry."

"What?" Rachael said, in a quiet, panicked tone. "You say you are carrying the *son of God?*"

"Yes, the Messiah I just spoke of is the one that I carry inside me, and it is surely the reason for the star that rests over your stable. I believe God sent you to me—and me to you—to fulfill the word of the prophets. And if I can teach you about God and persuade you that He is the one and only God in the universe, we will have added another soul to His kingdom."

As Joseph and Nathan entered the stable, they noted that the two women were deep in conversation.

Nathan said, "The talk of the town is about the star that hovers over our stable. Some are saying that it is a sign that a king is to be born." At that moment, the two women looked at each other knowingly. Nathan continued by saying, "I find it highly unlikely that a king would be born in a pathetic city like Bethlehem." And in a whispered voice, he added, "Bethlehem, Hebrew for 'the House of Bread'—right."

Joseph and Mary simply nodded at one another. Then Mary turned and looked at Rachael and smiled sweetly. That evening with Rachael's assistance, Mary gave birth to her firstborn child, Jesus, the Son of God, Joshua—which in Hebrew means 'God is salvation.'

And she wrapped Him in cloths, and laid Him in a manger, because there was no room for them in the inn (Luke 2:7b NASB).

After wrapping him in strips of cloth, Mary laid her infant son in the cattle trough lined with hay. Peering out into the night sky, the star shone brightly—twinkling brighter than before, over the roughhewn cradle where Jesus, the Lord of the universe, lay in sweet repose.

Meanwhile, Rachael shared with Nathan what Mary had told her. By God's grace and mercy, they both became believers of the one true God. And now, seeing this miraculous birth firsthand, both Rachael and Nathan simultaneously dropped to their knees to worship the child.

By his very birth, he changed lives, and this was only the beginning.

III

The Visiting Magi and the Peasant Boy

After coming into the house they saw the Child with Mary His mother; and they fell to the ground and worshiped Him. Then opening their treasures, they presented to Him gifts of gold, frankincense, and myrrh (Matthew 2:11 NASB).

Sometime later, as Jesus grew in strength in Bethlehem, magi from the East arrived in Jerusalem. They were asking where they could find the king of the Jews. When Herod, then king of Judea, heard of this, he summoned the magi, instructing them to find this new king and to report his exact location so that he could visit and worship him. The magi told King Herod only of the time the star had appeared. They then left him and went on their way, once again following the star.

Finally arriving in Bethlehem, the magi entered the stable and found baby Jesus. There they bowed down and worshiped him. They opened their sacks of treasures and presented the child with precious gifts of great value. Those included bags of pure gold, frankincense, and myrrh.

After their visit concluded, the magi prepared for their journey home. But having been advised in a dream to take a different route to their homeland, the magi left Jesus's cradle, ignoring the instructions of King Herod, and returned to Sipar via the southernmost route.

Mary and Joseph were a bit surprised that Jesus had been born into such a common place as the stable they now occupied. While they had never doubted the

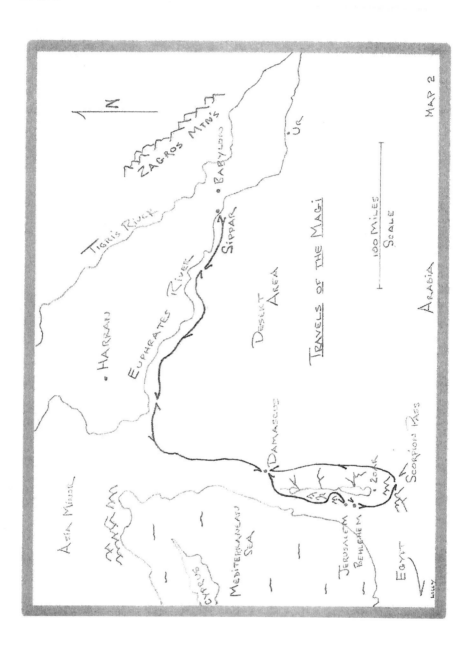

Lord or His direction, they found it comforting that the savior of the world had now been born. They were proud of baby Jesus, perfect in every way, and praised God for watching over them.

Surrounded by rough wood, animals, straw, and troughs of food for livestock, lay Jesus, the son of God. Here, in the humblest of places, Mary had encountered a pagan and shared God's truth with her. Rachael in turn had shared her newfound faith with Nathan, making him a believer as well.

As Mary thought about these things, she could not help but feel blessed and confused at the same time. She had been chosen above all other virgins to bring her own Savior into the world. When she looked adoringly into his eyes, she knew she was looking into the depths of creation, the universe, and quite literally into the face of God.

Even though his beginning was meager, he had already been worshiped by royalty—the magi from distant lands—and they not only came to see him but brought gifts of a value Mary could not even imagine. She and Joseph would pray about how these gifts should be used, for these treasures were only held by royalty or the affluent.

ⱺ℃℈✇⅋

As Mary dutifully watched over her infant son, she gazed again at the star. She caught a brief glimpse of what appeared to be someone looking in the window. She looked away, then back again, and this time was certain she had seen someone.

In Aramaic she said, "You may come in." And as Mary watched the open doorway, she saw a young peasant boy who was most likely seven or eight years of age. "Come in—you are welcome," Mary repeated in Aramaic.

The lad approached cautiously, and when he finally spoke, it was with a stuttering voice that he said, "Bu-bu-but I do not have a g-g-gift to bring, as the others did."

"Come closer; it's okay. This is Jesus," said Mary, "and he *is a gift* to *you* and all people. What is your name?"

"My n-n-name is Tadeo. They s-s-say he is the king," he said, pointing to Jesus. "Is th-th-that possible?"

Mary replied, "Tadeo, all things are possible with God."

As Tadeo knelt beside Jesus, he stumbled forward and, grabbing the edge of the manger, shook it slightly. It was just enough disruption to awaken the sleeping baby Jesus, who looked into the young boy's eyes. When Tadeo rose from the makeshift cradle, he looked at Mary and said, "He smiled at me—he smiled *at me*."

Mary could not help but notice the poor peasant boy was no longer stuttering. Through the smile of Jesus, a miracle had occurred. Mary knew in her heart, this was the first of many such inexplicable events in the life of Jesus the Christ.

IV

Visitors Galore

In the same region there were some shepherds staying out in the fields and keeping watch over their flock by night. And an angel of the Lord suddenly stood before them, and the glory of the Lord shone around them; and they were terribly frightened. But the angel said to them, "Do not be afraid; for behold, I bring you good news of great joy which will be for all the people; for today in the city of David there has been born for you a Savior, who is Christ the Lord. This will be a sign for you: you will find a baby wrapped in cloths and lying in a manger." And suddenly there appeared with the angel a multitude of the heavenly hosts praising God and saying, "Glory to God in the highest, and on earth peace among men with whom He is pleased." When the angels had gone away from them into heaven, the shepherds began saying to one another, "Let us go straight to Bethlehem then, and see this thing that has happened which the Lord has made known to us." So they came in a hurry and found their way to Mary and Joseph, and the baby as He lay in the manger. When they had seen this, they made known the statement which had been told them about this Child. And all who heard it wondered at the things which were told them by the shepherds. But Mary treasured all these things, pondering them in her heart. The shepherds went back, glorifying and praising God for all that they had heard and seen, just as had been told them (Luke 2: 8–20 NASB).

As word spread about town of the peasant boy's interaction with Mary and her baby, locals were asking each other what this could mean. They had seen the star and watched as the wealthy magi had ridden into town on their camels just to visit the stall of the innkeeper they knew as Nathan.

They now had heard of the shepherds' visit to the stall and heard *their* stories of angels and fulfilled prophecies.

The bravest of the townsfolk came to the stable and spoke with Joseph. He was usually found working off his debt to the innkeeper by repairing stalls, beams, and gates.

Mary and Joseph were naturally protective of the baby, but allowed any and all who would come to him to see him.

Some dropped to their knees after looking into the face of the child, while others simply wept tears of joy.

A seer named Arela entered the doors of the stable and spoke aloud of the pure-white aura she saw surrounding the child. She said she saw angels encircling the manger and fell to her knees so that she too could worship. She declared that this was *no ordinary* child. This was, as the prophets had said, the long-awaited king.

Farmers, astronomers, the curious, the meek, and the noble all came to see Jesus. Whether they came in reverence or out of sheer curiosity, they were all admitted and allowed to be in the presence of the blessed Child of God. Surely not one of these people left unchanged or unmoved. Each had been blessed, however unaware, to be in his presence.

V

The Trip to Egypt

Behold, an angel of the Lord appeared to Joseph in a dream and said, "Get up! Take the Child and His mother and flee to Egypt, and remain there until I tell you; for Herod is going to search for the Child to destroy Him." So Joseph got up and took the Child and His mother while it was still night, and left for Egypt (Matthew 2: 13–14 NASB).

The census required by Caesar Augustus was now complete. In a dream, an angel of the Lord made it clear to Joseph that it was time for them to leave Bethlehem and instructed them to go to Egypt as soon as possible.

Prior to leaving the inn of Rachael and Nathan, Mary and Joseph met with them to thank them for their kindness and pay for their lodging, food, and shelter. Nathan refused, pointing out the carpentry work Joseph had done in exchange for payment. Rachael agreed, telling Mary how the three of them had changed and improved their lives beyond measure.

Having predicted this reaction and having realized the dire circumstances of their finances, the couple had prayed about the indebtedness of the innkeeper. They had agreed the right thing to do was to pay them enough money to cover their outstanding debt. The two handed Nathan and Rachael a bag of gold that had been given to them by the magi. Joseph simply said, "Take this and use it to secure your inn. You gave us shelter when no one else would, and we will forever be grateful."

With heartfelt and tearful good-byes, the young family left Bethlehem and the humble stable where Jesus had been born. Just as they had arrived, they left under the cover of darkness, Mary atop the donkey, cradling baby Jesus in her arms, and Joseph guiding the donkey on the path.

Likewise shalt thou do with thine oxen, and with thy sheep: seven days it shall be with his dam; on the eighth day thou shalt give it to me (Exodus 22:30 KJV).

And when eight days were accomplished for the circumcising of the child, his name was called JESUS, which was so named of the angel before he was conceived in the womb (Luke 2:21 KJV).

Following the Law, all Jewish boys had to be circumcised on the eighth day after birth, and at six weeks of age, Mary and Joseph brought Jesus to the temple at Jerusalem where all firstborn Jewish males were to be presented to the Lord.

Mary and Joseph offered Jesus at the temple, where he was taken into the arms of the priest and lifted up before the altar. Jewish law signified this presentation as a solemn commitment and dedication to God. Jesus's name was then entered into the roll book that contained the names of the firstborn males of Israel.

Leaving the temple with Jesus, Mary and Joseph encountered Simeon, well known as a true servant of God. God had promised Simeon that he would not die until he had seen the Savior. And as soon as he saw the six-week-old Jesus, he *knew* this was the promised one. Simeon took Jesus into his arms, he praised God, saying that he could now die peacefully; he had seen the salvation of God in this young lad.

Mary thanked Simeon for his faithfulness to God and immediately left the temple garden with Joseph and Jesus. They had followed the law of registry and now needed to get on their journey to Egypt.

King Herod, realizing that he had been ignored and betrayed by the magi, made an edict to kill all boy children in Bethlehem two years of age and under.

Since the star of Bethlehem had first appeared a full two years before the actual birth of Jesus, and having been told of its original appearance, Herod would take no chance that he might leave the infant king alive.

ec C sc 2 eg

Now why go to Egypt to drink water from the Nile? And why go to Assyria to drink water from the Euphrates? (Jeremiah 2:18 NRSV).

The road to Egypt was long and arduous, stretching three hundred twelve miles (or five hundred two kilometers). The rocky roads, plus the sheer distance, had to be grueling for Mary, Joseph, and baby Jesus.

Early on in their journey, the three traveled alone. Joseph led the donkey that Mary rode on, and Mary held Jesus closely to her chest. The donkey was laden with their meager belongings as well. Traversing through Ramah, the roads were rocky and hilly.

Nearing a bluff, Joseph pulled back on the donkey, bringing him to a complete halt. Holding up his hand to signal Mary, Joseph simply nodded toward a man up ahead of them. With no alternative but to forge ahead, Joseph knew they would have to encounter him, and fearing an unpleasant exchange, urged Mary to hide baby Jesus as best she could.

As they came closer to the man, Joseph noticed he too had a woman in his company and saw that they appeared to be resting by the roadside. Mary took no chances, keeping Jesus tucked inside her wrap. As they approached the couple, the man waved to them.

While their tension was lessened after the initial friendly greeting, Mary was careful not to expose the baby. Upon meeting the couple, they learned they were travelers as well. Chatting for a few moments allowed the donkey to rest, all the travelers to sip some water, and Mary to loosen her hold and free Jesus from his hiding place.

When the couple saw Jesus, they were in awe of him and commented that he was a beautiful baby. Mary and Joseph thanked them and asked about their journey. They said they were bound for Gaza, where they hoped to meet up with a caravan of travelers going to Egypt.

Jennifer Taylor Wojcik
Philip G. Lilly D.Min.

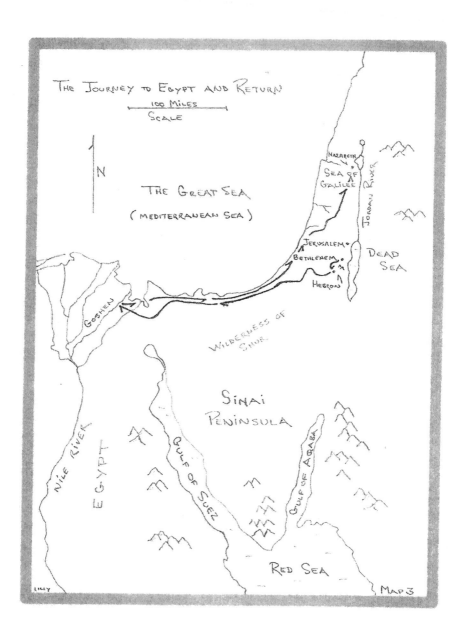

Since they were all headed to Egypt, Joseph asked if they might travel together to meet the caravan. The couple readily agreed and welcomed the company. Mary rode the donkey led by Joseph. She held Jesus close to her as they traveled, suckling him and tending to his every need.

Arriving in Gaza the next day, the two couples met with the caravan bound for Goshen in Egypt and began their sojourn surrounded by many other travelers. The caravan gave a sense of security and comfort to everyone, as there was safety in numbers.

Each night the travelers searched for whatever shelter they could find—a cave or crevice of stone that offered some protection from the elements—but still maintained close proximity to the rest of the caravan. The men would build fires inside a large circle so that the women could prepare communal meals. They shared their supplies so that no one went hungry or thirsty.

Reaching the border of Egypt would take several days, and though the baby Jesus was merely two months old, he was a well-behaved child. Fighting off exhaustion and weariness at times, Mary knew that everything would be fine for them, as long as they followed God's instruction. But looking at Joseph, she instinctively knew he was road weary and that his sandals needed to be replaced.

As the caravan approached a pool of still water, the group stopped, as they all were weary and worn from walking a great distance. As Joseph knelt to test the water, Mary saw that his feet were not only dirty but also covered in dried blood. His sandals were tattered and torn.

The water jugs were filled, thirsts were quenched, and the group opted to continue on for a few more hours. Joseph washed his feet, gently wiping the dried blood from them and donned a new pair of sandals, his last until he could make more.

Having seen his feet, Mary knew Joseph was exhausted, and so she opted to walk for a bit, allowing Joseph to rest by riding the donkey. While hesitant to do so and prepared to object, Mary was quite convincing. Mary, with Jesus held closely to her chest, had slipped off the donkey, taken the reins, and urged Joseph upward. Joseph rode for a while, resting his weary feet and legs and making his wife Mary happy.

Joseph, Mary, and Jesus were inconspicuous in the midst of the caravan, but virtually all the children in the company knew of Jesus and were impressed with him. They recognized something was different about him.

The children in the caravan had a natural affinity for Jesus and would bring him wild flowers they had picked along the roadside. One by one they would approach him, offering the flowers to him and all the while urging Jesus to give them a smile. Being a precocious child, Jesus readily handed out smiles.

Though always willing to share her time with others, Mary made Jesus her top priority. She held and nurtured him constantly. As they traveled toward Egypt, Mary talked to him, describing the sights they were experiencing on their journey.

She told Jesus about the Mediterranean Sea and the changing topography of desert, ocean, hills, and valleys they passed through. She related facts about Joseph, calling him "your father" and referred to him as a righteous man. She took pride in her husband, knowing that he had been chosen specifically for her. Joseph had stood by her, trusting in God, even when it was not easy to do so.

At bedtime, Mary, Joseph, and Jesus would lie down together and pray. Viewing the stars at night, Joseph would talk of the constellations and worlds beyond the sky, pointing out to Jesus that Our Father, the God of the universe, had created it all. As their prayer time ended, they would sleep peacefully, knowing that they were in the palm of the Father's hand—protected and loved.

At last, crossing the Nile, Joseph, Mary, and Jesus said farewell to the others remaining in the caravan. They were now approaching the northeast area of Egypt called Goshen.

The land of Goshen was a fertile region very close to the Mediterranean Sea. Family members of Joseph lived here and had been told by a messenger that their family was en route from Bethlehem. There, among friends and relatives, Mary, Joseph, and Jesus could begin a more normal family life together. There they could make a home, and Joseph could work.

Arriving in Egypt, Joseph took Mary and Jesus to his Uncle Hiram's house in Goshen. Joseph's extended family lived in the same compound and were excited about seeing him again and meeting Mary and Jesus. There would be feasts and parties planned to celebrate their reunion, but first there was the task of finding suitable housing in the compound for the family's newest arrivals.

While Joseph's family knew of Mary and Jesus, they were not yet privy to Mary's Immaculate Conception. Initially, no one spoke of the timing and circumstance of their marriage. And, as patriarch of the family, Hiram would be the person to address the issue with Joseph.

VI

Living in the Land of Goshen

But on that day I will deal differently with the land of Goshen, where my people live; no swarms of flies will be there, so that you will know that I, the Lord, am in this land (Exodus 8:22 NIV).

They also said to him, "We have come to live here for a while, because the famine is severe in Canaan and your servants' flocks have no pasture. So now, please let your servants settle in Goshen" (Genesis 47:4 NIV).

Jesus was immediately surrounded by love and attention from his extended family. Mary considered Jesus her mainstay—her purpose in life, and she doted on him. Aunts, uncles, and cousins made up the broadened family who adored being around him and made his life full.

Knowing her son was unique, and recognizing her task of raising Jesus as a tremendous responsibility, Mary tended to be overprotective of him. Joseph would gently urge Mary to share the boy with his family and allow him to play with and get to know his relatives.

Realizing that Joseph was right, Mary would relinquish her alone time with Jesus as he grew and matured from a baby to a young boy.

Having family members to rely on became a blessing, as cousins of Joseph referred him to townspeople for carpentry. Before long, Joseph was established in a shared carpentry shop with Hiram. As his handiwork now proved, he was more skilled than most, and his workload increased quickly. Joseph soon began teaching rudimentary carpenters how to make quality furniture and tools, as well as wheels and other equipment needed to make tasks easier.

With simple homes, mostly consisting of one or two-story dwellings, the people of Goshen tended to live in groups of three or more families, sharing a courtyard in the center of their houses. This common area allowed the women to make bread and cheeses and share harvested olives and grapes. It was also a safe area for the children to play with more than ample supervision from their extended family.

The top of the home dwelling was open air, but high enough to be free of stray animals, insects, and vermin. On warm nights, many families would sleep on the roof, using palettes of sackcloth as a bed.

The town of Goshen was blessed with a large community well of fresh drinking water. Built around the well was an area that became known as the market square. Women of the town would carry their jars there, some with the aid of their growing children, to fetch water and return to their family compound.

In the market square, there were rudimentary "shops" where townspeople or vendors would set up areas to sell their wares. There one could find hand-made cloth, rope, bins filled with grapes, cheeses, lentils, figs, and bottles of freshly extruded olive oil. Mary would often carry Jesus with her on her trips to the marketplace.

The local temple and synagogue were situated near the market square. There the local rabbi resided, giving counsel, holding religious ceremonies and rites, and teaching Jewish children the language and meaning of the Torah.

Situated in a prominent place in the square was Hiram's Carpentry, where Joseph now worked alongside his uncle. And it was in this carpentry shop that Joseph made Jesus his first pair of sandals.

Though he had never made a pair of shoes so small, Joseph took great pride in sanding down the soles of the sandals. He carefully placed holes for the soft rope to loop through to secure the sandals to the young boy's feet. Quite pleased with his work, he showed the sandals to Hiram.

"This is amazing workmanship—and all for one so small," Hiram commented.

Smiling at his uncle in appreciation, Joseph said, "Mary asked that I make Jesus a pair of sandals. While they won't get much use for a while, they are now ready for him to begin his journey through life."

While the market square was typically busy, on this particular day, Hiram unrolled the curtain to his shop, indicating that he was closed. Somewhat startled, Joseph asked, "Uncle, are we closing so early in the day?" Hiram simply nodded and walked to a wooden stool to sit closer to his nephew.

"Joseph, as the patriarch of our family, it is necessary that we discuss the circumstance of your marriage. Since you were recently married in Bethlehem, it is apparent that Mary was great with child before your wedding. It is my hope that you will explain how this occurred, as fathering a child out of wedlock is forbidden among our people."

Joseph smiled at Hiram, moving closer to him and sitting face to face with him. "Hiram, you are right to question this, and I have been remiss in not sharing these things with you before now. But it had to be the right time and under the right conditions for me to explain what has happened in my life and that of Mary and Jesus."

Hiram settled onto the stool and waited for Joseph to continue.

"The Lord of Heaven sent an angel to Mary, saying that she was the chosen virgin who would conceive God's son through the spirit of the most high and that she should name him Jesus. When she told me that, I was fearful and mistrusting at first, thinking that even though I was betrothed to her, I would simply marry and then divorce her," Joseph said.

"And is that your plan now, Joseph?" Hiram asked.

"No. An angel of the Lord came to *me* saying that it was God's will that Mary carry the child, assuring me that she had not been unfaithful. As a matter of fact, she and I married but did not have any sexual relations until after Jesus was born. So you see, both Mary and I have followed the will of our God, and I am honored to be the earthly father of Jesus."

Hiram shook his head in disbelief. "This is a very difficult thing for me to hear, Joseph. But I see that you are secure in your faith, and therefore I must believe that this has happened just as you say. Then this means that your son Jesus is the Son of God, the Messiah?"

"Yes. We have him in our care, and it is our responsibility to care for him, teach him the Law, and raise him to be what he is destined to be. It is that simple," Joseph responded.

"My nephew, there is nothing simple about this. You must be filled with fear that something untold will happen to him. We must share this revelation with the family so that extra care will be taken to protect Jesus."

"We can share our news with the family, but as God has promised, He will protect his own. We must simply facilitate that and educate Jesus as his heavenly Father instructs. We do not speak of these things in front of him. We don't even know if Jesus knows who he really is."

Joseph continued. "But, Hiram, he is already amazing. A young lad came to the manger shortly after Jesus's birth. He arrived with a marked stutter in his speech, and when he looked into the face of Jesus, Jesus smiled at him. The boy left speaking normally."

Joseph then related how the Lord had spoken to him in a dream and instructed him to take Mary and Jesus and come to Egypt. He explained that the king had decreed that every male aged two and under were to be put to death. "He made this proclamation in order to destroy our son. He had been told that a king greater than he had been born and would rule over all the earth. Had God not sent an angel to warn us, Jesus would have been slaughtered like all those other children."

Hiram arose and wrapped his arms around his nephew, holding him tightly. "We will support you, Mary, and baby Jesus in every way possible," he said. "Now let us go home and share this blessed story with the family. It is a time for celebration."

VII

Bless this House

Where the people of Israel were told, "For the Lord your God is the one who goes with you, to fight for you against your enemies, to save you." The officers also shall speak to the people saying, "Who is the man that has built a new house and has not dedicated it? Let him depart and return to his house, otherwise he might die in the battle and another man would dedicate it" (Deuteronomy 20:4 NASB).

With the story of Joseph, Mary, and baby Jesus related to the family via Hiram, a joyous celebration was planned. The local rabbi would be asked to give a blessing upon their home and upon the newest family living in Goshen.

The rabbi accepted Hiram's invitation and asked to meet with Joseph and Mary prior to the celebration so that he could get to know them.

Mary was most honored to have the rabbi in her new home. She prepared a special meal for him, and with the help of her new extended family, prepared a place for the group to dine together. The table was set for Hiram, the rabbi, and Joseph. Mary and Jesus would dine afterward.

That evening Jesus amazed the Rabbi. His good nature, inquisitive penetrating looks, and overall demeanor were beyond his earthly age. As the rabbi held him, Jesus looked directly into his face and smiled.

"He is a beautiful child," the rabbi said, "and seems so alert—as if he is taking everything in around him. Have all of our laws been followed since his birth?"

"Yes, Rabbi, he was circumcised on the eighth day and then presented at the temple in Jerusalem when he was six weeks old. There we presented him to the Lord and entered his name into the book," Joseph responded. "Jesus is our first child and has been dedicated to God."

"It is most excellent that you and your wife, Mary, follow the Law. But I am curious about why you would leave Bethlehem to make the journey to Goshen when you had such a young boy?" the rabbi asked.

Joseph explained King Herod's ruling to the Rabbi. "I was warned in a dream and told to come here," he said.

"A *dream?*" questioned the rabbi.

"Yes, the Lord spoke to me very clearly, urging me to take Mary and Jesus and come here for our safety," Joseph responded.

"I see," said the rabbi, who now had more questions than before.

Mary spoke up by saying, "Rabbi, we are followers of God and intend to do everything in our power to obey the laws set before us. When God spoke to my husband in a dream, we did not question the warning; we simply followed what we were told to do. God protected us on our journey, and we are blessed to be living in the land of Goshen."

"Well said, Mary. And your son appears to be perfect in every way. You indeed have been set apart. I will be most happy to offer up a blessing on you and your household."

The date and time was set, and preparations for the celebration began immediately.

Houses were looked upon as a gift of God and thereby needed to be dedicated according to the Law of Moses. When dedicating a new home, a Jewish blessing called the *shehecheyanu* is recited. That blessing says:

Blessed are You, Lord our God, King of the Universe, who has granted us life, sustained us, and enabled us to reach this occasion.

Obviously, the home of Joseph was quickly erected as an independent living space attached to the family homes already in the complex. Homes of that day were most often connected from one roof to another, with any gaps between them forming streets below. It was possible that one could run from rooftop to rooftop—for visiting certainly, but as a means of escape should one need it.

The home that Joseph's family was dedicating to God was basic, with a single large room subdivided for use by family and animals. The walls were thick, mostly made of mud or stone, and featured only a single window placed high up the wall to prevent unwanted entry. It was fitting to have a single-entry door, closed and secured with a wooden bar at night. Lighting sources were from oil lamps on the interior as well as the exterior. Additionally, there would have been both an interior and exterior stairwell that reached the roof.

The rooftop was covered with brushwood laid across sycamore beams, bound together with mud. Not impervious to weather because of its nature, the roof would have to be rolled to flatten the vegetation and in particularly rainy seasons were both lush in color and leaky.

Many hours of manual labor had resulted in this new house, and without exception, everyone in Joseph's extended family had done their part to make it happen.

Joseph, Mary and Jesus were comfortable in their new dwelling, thanking God daily for this latest blessing. Surrounded by Joseph's relatives, and yet having their own home, this newly created family relished their lives in Egypt. They were confident that they were living according to God's plan and prayed daily for continued guidance from their Father in heaven.

As the years passed, Mary and Joseph added to their family, giving Jesus two younger brothers.

VIII

The Return to Nazareth

After King Herod died, an angel of the Lord appeared to Joseph in a dream, instructing him to take Jesus, now about four years of age, and his mother, Mary, out of Egypt and to the land of Israel. The angel assured Joseph that those who were trying to kill Jesus were dead.

> *When Israel was a child, then I loved him, and called my son out of Egypt* (Hosea 11:1 KJV).

Joseph shared this news with Mary, and they immediately took Jesus and his two brothers back to Israel. They were fortunate to join a small caravan of travelers who were also en route to Israel. Now about five years of age, Jesus walked much of the route with his parents, but rode a donkey alongside Mary when he grew tired from walking.

At this curious age, Jesus asked many questions of his parents throughout the journey. He also now had a couple of siblings who required more of Mary's attention, so Jesus walked alongside Joseph.

As the caravan progressed, the travelers interacted more with one another, allowing their children to play together. Jesus loved the children his own age and enjoyed playing games with marbles and stones.

Often in the evenings they would gather around a fire and tell stories. The adults would make up stories they knew would interest the children. Keeping them in one place benefitted everyone, as storytelling would usually lull the young ones into sleep.

Jennifer Taylor Wojcik
Philip G. Lilly D.Min.

One night Jesus asked Joseph if he could tell a story. The adults agreed, so Joseph gave Jesus permission to tell his story. Jesus walked to the edge of the fire and began.

"Before I was born in Bethlehem, I lived in a completely different place. It was beautiful and filled with soft breezes and clear water. The air was fresh, and at times I felt like the clouds were underneath my feet like a cushion. There were animals of every kind, people of every nation, and I could hear soft music everywhere. There, no one was afraid. No one was hungry. If you had a question, there was always someone there to answer it. And if you wanted to play a game or sing a song, there was always someone there to play or sing with you. So now you are wondering why I didn't stay there, but came to Bethlehem instead? Sometimes I wonder too. All I know now is that this is where I am supposed to be, and I will just do my best as long as I am here. I also think that someday I will go back to the beautiful place I came from, but before I can do that, I have to serve my purpose here. I hope I can take all of you there with me, so you can see how beautiful it really is. Thank you for allowing me to tell my story."

The travelers applauded Jesus. Joseph and Mary looked to one another in amazement. At age five, what did the boy know?

Mary said, "That was a wonderful story, Jesus. Did you make it up?"

"I lived it, Mother," Jesus answered. "That's all I know."

During the journey, Joseph heard that Archelaus, son of Herod, was the new ruler in Samaria and Judea. The fact that a son of dreaded Herod was the leader made Joseph fearful. That could mean that settling in Bethlehem would be dangerous.

Again, warned by an angel of God in a dream, Joseph withdrew to the district of Galilee to settle in a town called Nazareth. Mary had previously lived in Nazareth and was familiar with the village recognizing it as a haven for the five of them. And so, it was there that Jesus grew up, living a quiet life with his family.

IX

Saul and Jesus

And the Child grew and became strong in spirit, filled with wisdom; and the grace (favor and spiritual blessing) of God was upon Him (Luke 2:40 AMP).

It was customary for young Jewish boys to begin attending school at about age six or seven. They would begin their scholastic life in what was called "the house of the book," where the Jewish religion and laws were available. Taught by a teacher who was paid by the synagogue, these men were required to be married and be of *good character.*

In their first years of training, the children were taught religion, designed to give them a better understanding of God. Elders in the faith would read from scrolls, while young boys would sit quietly in front of the teacher, trying to absorb every word. The elder would speak of what God had done, and particularly about God's laws, which had been handed down to Moses.

The school was attached to the Jerusalem temple, and beginning at age six, Jesus attended classes there and was recognized as a fast learner.

Most of the teaching was done by repetition and ultimately memorization by the students. It was the practice of the students to memorize their lessons then recite them aloud. After they were taught to write, the students took notes on a wooden tablet, marking it with a wax pen. Some students who didn't have tablets would write on the ground with a stick or stylus.

The only material used in the school was from the scrolls: the Law of Moses, the Writing of the Prophets, and Sacred Writings that later became the body of the Old Testament. Jesus, more often than not, was the first who volunteered to recite memorized lessons. All the teachers and scholars were amazed at his proficiency.

Saul, who later became known as Paul, was a Pharisee and attended the school in Jerusalem.

Pharisees were a powerful Jewish sect that observed a strict interpretation of the Law of Moses. Saul was a student at the same house of the book as Jesus. Being relatively close in age and in the same school, the two were bound to encounter one another.

Saul was a smart student—considered one of the brightest of the boys. Jesus was exceptionally sharp and well regarded by the elders and teachers. And while both Saul and Jesus retained knowledge easily, Jesus was prone to look beyond the sheer teachings of *fact,* for a *deeper,* more relevant meaning.

Saul had great confidence in his knowledge and like Jesus was one of the first to offer a recitation. He wore his self-assurance like a badge on his sleeve, and while pleasing to the instructors, many of his fellow students saw him as rigid and obnoxious.

One day, while Jesus was having a private conversation with his teacher, he asked questions that surprised and amazed the elder. Saul, standing nearby, overheard the dialogue and began to explain his position on the subject by quoting text from the scrolls.

"Thank you, Saul," said Jesus. "I now know where you stand on the issue, but I would very much like for the elder to share his thoughts and his reasoning." Jesus smiled at Saul and turned back to the teacher.

Saul did not like being ignored, nor left out of the conversation. "But, Jesus, I have given you the answers you seek, haven't I, Teacher?"

The elder spoke gently to Saul, saying, "Your answer is correct in the strictest sense of the word. I believe Jesus is asking me to go a step beyond the literal explanation and is asking for my opinion and interpretation. Is that correct, Jesus?"

"Yes, Teacher. It is your opinion and belief that I seek," Jesus said.

"Humph," said Saul as he turned and walked away. Under his breath he uttered, "I was right, and he knew it."

That encounter with Saul and Jesus was only the first of three that followed as the boys became men and each fulfilled their destinies.

X

The Marketplace

"To what can I compare this generation? They are like children sitting in the marketplaces and calling out to others..." (Matthew 11:16 NIV).

The marketplace was used by everyone in the village, and some frequented it more often than others. The market was the place where the village water supply could be easily accessed by the townspeople who brought jars and jugs to fill and tote home. James, now eight years old, and Joses, now seven years old, would accompany their mother, Mary, to the marketplace to assist her in carrying home water, figs, or supplies. The younger children—Judah, Simon, and baby Miriam—would stay with relatives in the family complex.

Young children would often accompany their parents, where they mixed and mingled with other children as well as the merchants. Wide-eyed kids were amazed at the colorful carts, draped with textiles or laden with fruit. The activities and noises of the marketplace were never the same from day to day but were always of interest. Jesus, who had just celebrated his tenth birthday, walked to the market alongside one of his friends, whose name was Chision. With no particular agenda, the two friends just wanted to see what was happening in the marketplace. It was always colorful, ever changing, and offered great opportunities to people watch. As usual the market was bustling with activity, from local villagers who had brought in *their* produce to the daily influx of traders from the surrounding area.

It was a safe enough place—happy by all accounts and a great way to experience life outside of school or home. It was certainly an enlightening experience due to the products that were available and the variety of merchants that came there to set up shop.

Much like any place where groups gathered, there were the not-so-nice kids who hung out in groups that would now be referred to as gangs. And of course, Jesus and Chision met up with just such a clique.

Chision was regarded as being unintelligent, useless, and physically unattractive—a dorky sort by all accounts. Jesus didn't look at Chision in that light, but rather thought of him as someone who not only needed but deserved a friend.

As the clique approached them, they began to taunt Chision. Having had this experience more than once, Chision immediately put himself in a safer position—behind Jesus.

In a kind but firm voice, Jesus asked, "What's going on with you guys? Why do you call my friend names and make fun of him?"

"You need to pick better friends, Jesus," said one young lad. "This guy is a loser, and everyone knows it except you."

Another clique member pushed forward. "He's dumb, and we don't like him. He's so dumb he probably can't even find his way home from the market. That's probably why you came with him, right?" taunted the boy.

Laughing louder than all the others, he continued. "You had to come with him so he could make it back home?" The group broke up in laughter, slapping their sides and pointing to the now embarrassed and fearful Chision.

Jesus inched a step closer to the group. "Chision is my friend. His very name means 'hope and trust,' and I have chosen him to be my friend. Are you angry that I chose him?" Jesus asked.

"Nah—we don't care who your friends are; we just thought you were smarter than that. You should hang around with cool guys, you know?"

"So you guys are all alike and, as you say, cool?" Jesus asked. "And you want all your friends to be just like you are—making fun of someone just because they are *different* from you? Why would anyone want friends who are like that?"

Jesus continued, putting an arm around Chision. "We are all different, and each of us has a place in the grand scheme of things. God made us each unique, giving us talents, strengths, and shortcomings as well. Have you not heard this at the synagogue? Do you think you are so special that learning the laws of God aren't important?"

Jesus saw one boy in the rear of the pack looking nervous and uneasy. "You there," said Jesus, "how about you? Do you think you are like your friends?"

Sheepishly the boy said, "No, and I don't want to be like them; they're not really my friends either."

"Then leave the group and find friends you can count on and trust," Jesus said. "Come and spend some time with Chision and me. You will have made the better choice, and you will be respected as a friend."

The young man left the clique amid jeering and laughter. "Traitor," they taunted.

Jesus replied, "He was not disloyal to you. He has instead opted to follow the truth. He can now count on his real friends—with hope and trust."

XI

Jesus the Sculptor

For the Most Holy Place he made a pair of sculptured cherubim and overlaid them with gold (2 Chronicles 3:10 NIV).

Not long after, and during a school break, Jesus began spending a great deal of time in Joseph's carpentry shop. Not only was Jesus learning the trade of his father, he was also allowed to make his *own creations* from leftover wood. Because of his eye for detail, he would often pick up scraps from the bin and independently work with them. This fostered not only Jesus's creativity, but his competency as well.

After Jesus finished the work Joseph had for him, he rummaged through the bin of scraps, finding a gnarly piece of acacia wood, more commonly known as gum arabic. Jesus politely asked Joseph's permission to use the knotted wood. Joseph of course agreed.

"When I look at this piece of wood, I see a bird," Jesus told Joseph.

Jesus's brother James, who had recently been spending time in the carpentry shop, stopped sweeping and looked at his brother. "You see a what? The last thing I see in that scrap of wood is a bird!"

"I don't see that, son," said Joseph to Jesus, "but by all means, bring the bird out of the wood."

Jesus held the entangled wood up to the light, visualizing what it might become. He immediately gathered the tools he would need and started to work on the piece of acacia wood.

Carving the wood with a chisel and rasp was time consuming, but it helped him achieve just the results he wanted. By midafternoon Jesus had carved a bird with outstretched wings created from the scrap of wood.

"Wow," said James. "I can almost see it flying out of here!"

Joseph stood amazed. "What a beautiful bird, son. What are you going to do with it? Would you like to take it home for the other children to see?"

"It is a dove—a bird of peace. I would like to place the dove here on the window sill, Father, so that everyone who passes by can see," Jesus answered.

Joseph responded, "That is a fine idea, son."

Jesus carefully placed the wooden dove on the window sill. After admiring his son's handiwork, Joseph left for home with Jesus and James.

When the three came to the carpentry shop the next day, the dove was gone.

"I don't know what could've happened to your carved bird," Joseph said.

"I know, Father" said Jesus. "As a piece of scrap wood, it had no life. But by making it new again, giving it love and purpose, it was transformed and surely flew away, carrying the message of peace as it was intended."

"You can create another if you would like," said Joseph.

"But no two doves are alike, Father. It would not be the same. While we are all wonderfully made, no two people are exactly the same. We see things differently. While I saw a dove with its wings outstretched, someone else may have only seen a gnarly piece of wood. The creator sees what could be and allows it to be. Perhaps someone needed that piece of wood for another reason and took it. If so, then the dove and the wood have fulfilled their purpose."

"That's silly," said James. "Wooden birds can't fly, can they, Father?"

"Only those who are filled with life," said Joseph.

XII

Jesus in the Temple

"Why were you searching for me?" He asked. Didn't you know I had to be in my Father's house?" (Luke 2:49 NIV).

Every year for Passover, Mary and Joseph traveled to Jerusalem to celebrate the holiday. Along with his brothers and sisters, Jesus would accompany them on these annual pilgrimages, enjoying being part of the caravan of travelers as much as the celebration.

The year Jesus was twelve, they made the trip as usual, but once it had ended and they were on their way home, they realized that Jesus was nowhere to be found among the caravan crowd. Mary and Joseph asked Jesus's siblings if they had seen him. None of them had seen him since they left Jerusalem.

More than concerned about Jesus's safety, they placed Jesus's siblings in the charge of family and left the caravan to return to Jerusalem. There they searched for him for three long, grueling days. When the anxious parents found him in the temple—sitting among Israel's foremost scholars—they were, to say the least, relieved.

Not only was their son listening intently to these scholars, he was asking them thought-provoking questions. Amazed at the depth of knowledge this young man had, these holy men, known as experts in Hebrew Scriptures, were awed by the boy. Jesus was responding to the elders' questions with clarity and purpose, awing even the most learned of holy men.

Jennifer Taylor Wojcik
Philip G. Lilly D.Min.

When Mary asked Jesus why he disappeared, Jesus asked why she was looking for him since he had to be about his Father's business, in his Father's house. But after having said that, he respectfully returned home to Nazareth with his family, leaving behind quite an impression on the religious scholars at the temple.

On the outskirts of Jerusalem, Jesus noted a crowd had gathered just off the main road. There had been no mention of this by Mary or Joseph. When Jesus asked what the mass of people had gathered for, Joseph explained that there had been trials going on throughout the prior week.

"But what sort of trials?" asked Jesus.

"When people break the Law, they are captured and tried in the religious court or that of the Romans. Some are found guilty and suffer a penalty as a result. It appears there is a punishment being enacted on someone who was found guilty," Joseph replied.

"May we go closer?" Jesus asked, with slight hesitancy in his voice. "I cannot see from here."

Mary responded to her son's plea. "Jesus, punishment exacted under the Law is not something I would care for you to see. We've been delayed on our journey already and should be headed back home. Your brothers and sisters are with their aunts, and we should be getting home to them. Besides, it's not a pretty sight to see someone beaten, stoned, or worse."

"Please, Mother," said Jesus. "I am eager to learn about these and all things that pertain to the Law. We do not need to stop there; passing close by will suffice."

Joseph agreed to take a slightly different route and pass by the area where the crowd had gathered.

As they neared the site, Jesus could clearly see a man was being flogged with a whip-like contraption that had many straps made of leather with sharp objects on each end. With each blow, blood gushed out of the man's skin, and he was struck repeatedly.

Mary turned her eyes away and Joseph kept the donkey moving onward. Jesus stared at the flogging. Mary noticed her son's visible shudder each time the strips of leather and barb tore at the man's flesh. It was as if Jesus felt every blow that was struck.

Jesus quietly said to his parents, "This man must be guilty of horrible crimes to receive such punishment; surely an innocent man would not be so mistreated or judged unfairly." Jesus remained silent and contemplative during the rest of their journey home.

XIII

The Blind Lady

As Jesus had often done before, he accompanied his mother into the market square. Today he would help his mother by carrying her purchases and the water jugs home from the market's well.

Mary and Jesus encountered a blind woman named Eleora who was shopping at a local vendor's stand. Mary knew the woman and greeted her.

"Are you well, Eleora?" asked Mary.

"I am well, thank you," said the woman. "I've just come to purchase some figs and grapes from the market. I've heard the ones here are sweet and fragrant."

Mary then introduced her son Jesus to Eleora so that she would know who stood before her.

"Hi, Eleora," said Jesus. "It is a pleasure to meet you."

"And you," said Eleora as she turned toward Jesus. "You must be your mother's pride and joy. Your voice is so calming, caring. I can sense the kindness in your tone, even though I cannot physically see you."

"Thank you, ma'am," said Jesus, with a smile. "I will leave you to your shopping." He then walked around the crates of merchandise and noticed there were two sets of scales kept by the merchant; one on top of the coin box, the other kept out of sight underneath a set of empty crates.

When Eleora had gathered her figs in one cloth and her grapes in another, she made her way to the merchant to pay for her fruit.

Jesus saw that the merchant was about to weigh the fruit on the hidden scale. He simply stepped forward quietly, touched the woman's hand, and whispered in her ear, "Ask if he treated you fairly or if he perhaps made a mistake in weighing your fruit. Please, just ask."

As Eleora asked this of the merchant, Jesus moved to him and touched his arm gently. The merchant gasped at the mere touch of Jesus. He then looked into the face of Jesus and turned to the woman, saying, "Oh, ma'am, forgive this old merchant. I may have mistakenly overcharged you. Please take the figs free of charge today to make amends for my error."

"Thank you, sir," said Eleora. "Have a blessed day."

"Have a blessed day, Eleora" said Jesus as he reached out again to the merchant, this time clasping his hand. He then smiled at the seller and walked away, saying nothing more.

Jesus watched and noted that the demeanor of the merchant was now changed. He was moving the errant scales out of reach, putting them underneath his table, not to be used again. Jesus heard him greeting the next customer with a kinder, soothing tone in his voice.

"Today is a blessed day, Mother," Jesus said as Mary nodded.

"You have been a positive influence on that charlatan," Mary said, "and Eleora was treated fairly thanks to your intervention. You are wise beyond your youthful years, my son, and I am pleased."

"People should be treated fairly, with respect and kindness. Those people with infirmities should not be abused because of them. You have always taught me to be courteous, kind, and honorable. Perhaps that merchant's mother did not teach him those lessons."

XIV

The First Wound

For the life of a creature is in the blood, and I have given it to you to make atonement for yourselves on the altar; it is the blood that makes atonement for one's life (Leviticus 17:11 NIV).

A father shared his trade with his children to perpetuate the craft and to insure the children were trained and equipped to provide for their future families.

Joseph was an exceptional carpenter, with extraordinary skills others longed to have. Many carpenters of the day made simple objects, such as doors, furniture, and eating utensils, while Joseph was accomplished in creating wooden wheels—a precise and complicated project that contributed greatly to the emerging transportation methods. Joseph had learned this skill by emulating his father.

Just as Joseph's father had taught *him*, he had been teaching Jesus carpentry since Jesus was a young boy. As expected, Jesus was a quick learner, taking Joseph's instruction readily and closely following Joseph's direction. Before age twelve, he had learned the basics of carpentry as well as the use of all the basic tools.

Joseph had started by teaching Jesus the fundamentals of his craft, adding more information and showing him more skilled techniques over time. Beginning with the tools of the trade, Joseph described each implement as well as their specific function.

Jesus learned that the early tools used in woodworking and carpentry included saws, usually manned by two workers that cut on the "pull" stroke and were particularly useful in cutting down trees and sawing pieces of wood in two. Joseph showed Jesus both the ax and adz, which were used for cutting, carving, and shaping wood.

Joseph's shop included an assortment of mallets, chisels, and handmade drills used for adding detail or attaching pieces together. Bow drills, resembling a bow and arrow, were used for drilling holes in wood planks. The arrowhead was positioned against the plank and used to bore the hole. Though elementary and tedious, the bow drill eventually got the job done.

As a carpenter progressed in his skill, he would often create wheels for wagons and carts. These techniques were both time consuming and significantly more advanced.

Because Jesus was now older and more experienced in carpentry, Joseph explained to him that in order to have the proper materials to work with, a carpenter had to learn about the many types of trees. Joseph not only taught his son how to recognize the *kinds* of trees but how to cut them down in order to preserve the tree for future growth. From that point, Jesus learned how to square up logs and then hone the timber into usable sizes based on its intended use.

Cutting down trees required the use of a hand adz—or by hand sawing the breadth of the timber, then sawing the length of it. Typically, Joseph would purchase rough lumber that had already been harvested from the forest, but it was important that his son understand the process and to recognize that, regardless of the method, it was hard physical work.

Requiring skill and precision, carpentry was part science, part art. With Joseph's guidance, Jesus was becoming more and more proficient. By age fifteen, Jesus had developed most of the skills that Joseph had exhibited and was a more-than-able carpenter. His strength often appeared boundless, and his eye for detail and the artistic side of the craft was obvious to anyone who saw his work.

The awl—a sharply pointed and round-end blade with a handle—was Jesus's favorite tool because he could make precisely positioned holes in pieces of wood.

Jesus worked hard to not only please Joseph but to feel a great sense of pride in his accomplishments. He was meticulous and exacting in all that he attempted, so the day he accidentally stabbed himself with the awl, he was stunned, and Joseph was beside himself.

The clamp holding the wheel that Jesus and Joseph were working on unexpectedly lost its grip, and the awl Jesus was using to start a hole in the wheel jammed into his hand.

Blood poured from Jesus's palm. Joseph immediately went to his son's aid, tearing off a section of cloth from his own garment and wrapping it around his son's bleeding hand. Jesus was calmly observing the wound as Joseph bound his hand.

Jesus said, "Father, I am fine."

"But, son, there is much blood coming from this wound. Here, this should help stop the bleeding," Joseph said as he tended to his son's hand, applying a slight pressure to the gushing wound.

Moments later Jesus removed the bandage and held out his hand to Joseph. "See, Father? The bleeding has stopped."

Joseph took the hand of Jesus and noted that a pool of blood had formed in the center of his palm. "It looks very serious to me," said Joseph. "It appears the awl pierced the palm of your hand."

Jesus eyed his pierced palm and answered, "This wound will heal, Father, and perhaps even leave a scar to remind me of today, but it will not be the last time I suffer wounds as I go about the work that is before me. Every wound and scar that I receive will serve as a reminder of the purpose I have been given."

XV

The Little Fat Girl

She was a quiet young girl; some said she was chunky, and others just called her fat. Many of the kids in her small village of Magdala would push her around and call her ugly names. She was a bit shorter than most of the kids her age, which made her weight more obvious.

Her Hebrew name was Miryam, which translated meant "fat one." Later in life she would be referred to as Mary Magdalene, named for the small, quiet fishing village where she was born.

Like many of the children of the Jews living outside the kingdom of Israel, her parents were of mixed races. Her father, Areal, was Jewish and stated clearly that he was from the tribe of Asher. Her mother, Rhonda, on the other hand, claimed that her family was originally from the city of Tyre, on the Mediterranean. Rhonda came from a family of fishermen and was considered an outsider by many of her Jewish neighbors in Magdala.

At about age three, Mary's mother noticed that she would often slip into moments of quiet withdrawal. At other times Mary would become physically erratic and uncontrollable. Aging didn't help the behavior, and as Mary grew older, her siblings would avoid her, as if she didn't exist.

As the cycles of quiet and frenzied progressed, so did the estrangement from her siblings and to some degree, her parents. Neighbors quietly whispered that the behavior by Mary was punishment by God on this family for Areal's failure to have followed the Law of Moses since he had married outside the faith.

Early in his life, Mary's father, Areal, worked in the local basalt mines. Basalt stones were chiseled out of the nearby hillsides and then shaped into grinding stones that were then used to grind barley, wheat, and other local and regional grains into flour. More importantly the stone wheels were used to press precious oil out of olives.

Later in life Areal progressed from being a miner of the stones to that of a cutter and shaper who crafted the rough stones into round wheels and milling base plates. Opening his own business, Areal became successful. It was hard work, and he worked long hours, but he provided an excellent living in support of his family.

In late November Areal and the family decided to travel to Nazareth to visit relatives. Nazareth was roughly forty kilometers southwest of Magdala, and the trip would take the family two days to complete.

Their Nazareth relatives lived near Mary, Joseph, and their children. As one would expect, the children from both families quickly found each other and began to mingle and play. Within a few days, the parents of both families met and began chatting, sharing, and eventually eating together. Areal and Rhonda quickly found Jesus to be an exceptionally bright and charming young man. In Jesus, they saw an opportunity and within days acted on that prospect.

Following a common practice of the time, Mary Magdalene's parents approached Jesus's parents and proposed a future marriage between Jesus and Mary.

The marriage offer had caught them off guard. Mary and Joseph quickly, but gently, closed the conversation and at the same time expressed their appreciation for the offer. Once alone they expressed concerns to one another about Mary's emotional stability.

Both Joseph and Mary decided it best to approach Jesus about the subject, and they went directly to him to seek his thoughts. As they began the conversation, Jesus listened carefully, smiling and nodding his head. At the end of the conversation, he said to his parents, "May I have your permission to go directly to Mary and her parents to discuss this matter?" They agreed.

Mary's parents listened as Jesus spoke with them, showing the appropriate respect for their suggested involvement with Mary. As she sat nearby, she listened intently but did not fully understand what was taking place. Jesus explained his mission in great detail, explaining he was to follow the will of God. Areal understood Jesus's position, but as a pagan, Rhonda heard nothing beyond rejection.

While talking with Mary's parents, Jesus sensed that Mary was moving into a manic state. He stepped over to her and gently took her by the hand. She was immediately calmed. Her parents saw this and were astonished. To them, this act only reinforced their conviction that Jesus and Mary needed to be a couple.

As the conversation continued, Jesus recognized that Mary's parents were under the assumption that he was being called to be a rabbi or priest, which would not necessarily deter the marriage. Realizing as well that the time had not yet come to *fully* explain his mission on earth, Jesus concluded the conversation with Mary's parents by asking permission to speak with her one-on-one.

Outside the austere house, Jesus turned to Mary and began to speak. "You are a beautiful young woman, Mary, and the course of your life will take many twists and turns. Yet in the end you will be blessed and have your heart's desires. I am certain that our paths will cross again. I pray that you will be there and that you will be ready to respond. I will need you."

No doubt Mary did not fully understand or comprehend what Jesus was saying. But as they parted she felt a great relief and warmth inside. Explaining only that she and Jesus were truly friends and that their paths would cross again, Mary told her parents she was ready to go home. The next day Mary and her family departed Nazareth for the trip back to Magdala.

More than two years had passed since their trip to Nazareth. The lives of Mary, her parents, and her siblings had moved on. By this time in her life, Mary had unfortunately gained a reputation as a flirtatious and poorly behaved girl, and her life was about to begin a downward spiral.

Late one night an unusually heavy rainstorm developed over the Sea of Galilee. The storm crept ashore and eventually hit Magdala. While it was not uncommon for a large storm to come off the sea and engulf Magdala, they would usually dissipate quickly. This storm was different. As the storm began to unleash its fury, water quickly started to run deep in the streets.

A loud crashing noise startled and awakened Areal. Opening the shutters on the window, he could see that the house next door had partially collapsed from the torrent of water streaming down what was formerly the street running between the two houses.

Acting purely on instinct, Areal ran out the door and headed directly into the downpour and his neighbor's house. He had not taken the time to put on his sandals or cloak. Just as he was about to reach the front of his neighbor's house, his bare feet lost their traction, and he was swept away with the rushing water.

Moments later Areal's house collapsed, killing everyone except Mary. She was found the next morning shivering yet still clinging to a post just outside the door where their house once stood. Areal's body was never found, and it was assumed that he had been washed out to sea.

At the time of the tragedy, Mary was just old enough to marry. A relative living in the area offered to marry her, but she declined. Shortly after her declination, she sold the family business to that relative, which left her wealthy but still dealing with the ravages of her mental state and apparent sexually promiscuous tendencies.

XVI

Special Delivery

"Suppose someone has enough to live and sees a brother or sister in need but does not help. Then God's love is not living in that person. My children, we should love people not only with words and talk, but by our actions and true caring" (1 John 3:17–18 NIV).

More often than not, part of the job of carpentry involved delivery of the finished piece(s) to the customer.

Joseph and Jesus had just completed making a wagon wheel for a customer from a neighboring village. Leaving James, Joses, and Judah at the carpentry shop with Joseph, Jesus left the shop midmorning to deliver the wheel to its owner, who lived in Kfar HaHoresh.

Carefully lifting the heavy wooden wheel onto the donkey, Jesus made sure to distribute its weight evenly to lessen the burden of the animal that carried it. Cinching woven straps underneath the donkey, Jesus tested the security of its tether. Once satisfied that all was well with the animal, Jesus made his way down the dirt road that connected Nazareth to Kfar HaHoresh. This particular roadway was fairly well traveled, but on this particular day, foot traffic was sparse.

As Jesus made his way closer to town, he came upon a local olive grower whose cart was stuck in a stream he had attempted to cross. Carefully, Jesus walked his donkey down from the road toward the stream and allowed him to drink from the water as he approached the olive grower.

"Need a helping hand, sir?" Jesus asked.

"Yes, I fear I am in need of assistance," said the grower. "The load is heavy, and my wheels are mired in the stream's bed."

"I am happy to help," said Jesus. "My name is Jesus; what is yours?"

"Jesus, I am called Iri," answered the grower. "I am blessed that you came along and have offered to help."

"I would suggest we take the heavy vats of oil off the cart," said Jesus. "That will lighten the load. We should then be able to free the cart and your donkey, and we can reload the oil on firmer ground."

Jesus and Iri worked side by side removing the vats of oil and carefully placing them on the ground. Chatting as they worked, Jesus asked the grower about his crop.

"Tell me about the oil," said Jesus.

"Ah, my new friend, the oil is a gift from God. My family has been growing olive trees for generations. Do you know how the trees are planted and how they grow?" asked Iri.

"I would love to hear about it while we work," said Jesus.

"I come from a long line of olive growers. My great-grandfather grafted a tree that he had cultivated into a wild stock—just from a tiny olive vine. He would then cut it down to the ground. The roots would begin to grow deep into the earth and take hold. The new shoots would then be grafted into more stock, and it continued until our fields were filled with olive trees."

Barely stopping for a breath, Iri continued. "While it takes many years for a tree to reach its maturity, once it does, the tree will bear fruit for many, many years to come."

"We light our torches and lamps by adding a wick to the olive oil," Jesus commented.

"Ah, yes," said Iri, "the oil has many uses, and I was named Iri because it means 'fire light.' Some of the oil derived from our fields has been used for anointing prophets and kings who are in God's service. That is why I know the olive tree and its production are truly a gift of God." Iri continued his explanation as they worked. "These olives have been picked at their peak ripeness to be processed through the press. Have you ever seen an olive press?"

Jesus answered, "No, I have not."

"The press we use is a large round stone with a trench carved into it. We place the fruit in the trench, then with a smaller stone attached to a wooden board, we roll the smaller stone over the olives to crush them. Once we have that pulp, we squeeze the oil out of them, place it in jars, and allow the sediment to separate from the oil. The top of the oil is the purest and the best of the lot; it actually comes from the first turn of the olives. Subsequent turns produce a slightly different quality of oil. It is really quite a process."

Jesus asked Iri, "Is this the way your grandfather produced olive oil as well?"

"Yes," said Iri, "but their process of pressing the oil was different. My ancestors used a smaller stone press and literally rolled the smaller stone around the press by hand. By making the press larger and attaching the plank, we learned we could produce more oil in a shorter amount of time."

"So your best oil is reserved for royalty?" asked Jesus. "And the prophets spoke of a messiah who is yet to come," said Jesus, "and he would be the anointed one, correct?"

"Yes, sir, that is correct," Iri said. "And it is my prayer that the Messiah be anointed with the oil of our fields."

Jesus nodded, smiling.

By the time Iri had finished his story, he and Jesus had completely unloaded the cart so that it could be pulled free.

"Let's tie a rope to my donkey and the cart. He will help us pull the cart free from the mire." Jesus led the donkey over to Iri and freed the trapped cart.

Reloading the cart was quick work for the two.

"You, sir, have done me a great favor," Iri said.

"And you have been a most interesting man. I wish you well in your fields and on your journeys." As he spoke, Jesus noted the sun was setting in the west. "We must move quickly, my friend, so that both of our tasks can be finished before dark."

Iri responded, "Thank you—I owe you a great debt."

Jesus simply smiled at Iri, gathered his donkey, and made his way toward Kfar HaHoresh.

XVII

Jesus, The Sheepherder, and the Lion

Then David said to Saul, "Your servant was tending his father's sheep. When a lion or a bear came and took a lamb from the flock, I went out after him and attacked him, and rescued it from his mouth; and when he rose up against me I seized him by his beard and struck him and killed him." (1 Samuel 17:34–35 NASB).

When Jesus was roughly eighteen, he was walking along the road en route to his home. He had just delivered a completed carpentry project for Joseph and was headed home for the evening meal when the sound of a distraught animal caught his attention. Stopping, he looked around the cavernous hillside, where he spotted a lamb alone and in distress.

Hearing the bleating of a sheep, Jesus noticed that a lone ewe had wandered off from its herd. Now looking around for the shepherd, he found that the sheepherder was nowhere in sight.

While Jesus knew that sheep were prone to wander, he also knew that they could rarely survive without the shepherd's care and protection. As he thought about the lamb's misery, he noticed a lion in the distance that had also heard the bleating of the sheep and was now bounding toward it at a great speed.

Cupping his hands to his mouth, he cried out, "Shepherd, Shepherd! A lion is about to attack your sheep! You must come quickly to save your sheep!" But as he looked all around, Jesus heard nothing except the echo of his own voice rising from the desert floor.

Without hesitation Jesus ran and intercepted the lion, striking his head with a stick—stunning him, allowing the sheep a brief reprieve.

Jesus instinctively knew that without further action, he would be observing the lion as he caught and killed his prey. "Please, Father, show me the lesson I am to learn from this terrible sight," Jesus uttered.

The sheepherder arrived too late. When he finally arrived, he wept, saying, "Ah, my sheep, my sheep." The sheep was being torn apart and eaten hungrily and quickly by the ravenous lion. There was nothing more he could do but watch and be saddened by his loss.

Jesus said, "I called for you, Shepherd, but you were tending to your other flock and did not come to the aid of the stray. My Father tells me the lesson is that if but one of your flock goes astray, you, as the shepherd, must make every effort to rescue it, lest the one who goes astray will surely be devoured."

When Jesus reached his home, he felt compelled to tell his brothers and sisters about what had happened.

Lydia, now age eight, and Assia, age nine, both shed tears for the poor lost sheep. Though Miriam was only a year older, she ushered the girls back into the kitchen area of the house, speaking softly to them and urging them not to cry. She explained that the sheep was no match for the lion and fell prey to it as a result of wandering alone.

The boys were more interested in hearing about how Jesus struck the beast on the head, risking his own life to stun the lion in hopes of saving the sheep.

Jesus repeated the lesson he learned so that his brothers would also understand.

Be of sober spirit, be on the alert, the devil prowls around like a roaring lion, seeking someone to devour (1 Peter 5:8 NASB).

XVIII

Up on the Roof

As high as the sky is above the earth, so great is His love for those who respect Him. He has taken our sins away from us as far as the east is from the west. The Lord has mercy on those who respect Him, as a father has mercy on his children. He knows how we were made; He remembers that we are dust (Psalm 103:11–14 NIV).

Since houses were constructed with an open-air roof, not only were the cool breezes prevalent, but the view of the entire sky was looming.

During warmer months, many families would move their sleeping quarters to the rooftop, taking advantage of the coolness as well as being separated from the odiferous animals that were also kept in the dwelling.

With the winter season swiftly approaching, Jesus opted to go up to the roof. It was well after midnight, and while he would normally have been sleeping, he felt compelled to go up on the roof.

Jesus had just turned twenty years of age and had grown in wisdom and knowledge that surpassed everyone's expectations. He had been thinking of taking a journey to see other parts of the world, outside the safety and sanctity of his home and family.

Slipping on his sandals, Jesus carefully left his bed and approached the stairway. He quietly climbed to the rooftop, hoping not to wake anyone else in the family. As he topped the stairway, Jesus looked upward, seeing the sky that revealed a stunning display of the celestial stars. It was a breathtaking view indeed and one that he had always had a penchant for watching.

Jennifer Taylor Wojcik
Philip G. Lilly D.Min.

Jesus had spent only a few minutes there before his mother discovered he was not in his bed and came looking for him. As she peered over the edge of the rooftop, she saw Jesus lying on his back, looking upward into the vast array of stars. "Jesus? It is so late, and I feared for your safety. Why are you here on the roof in the cold?"

"Ah, my sweet mother," said Jesus. "I am studying my Father's handiwork. His creation is marvelous, and I cannot think of anyone who could doubt His existence in light of this beauty."

Mary took a seat next to Jesus. "I know, son, I too marvel at God's handiwork and am prone to wonder why I was blessed to be an integral part of the Father's plan. But you should know, Jesus, that I thank Him daily for choosing me."

"You do not speak of it often," said Jesus, "but I sense your thankfulness and feel your awe. But tonight is special. As I gazed up at the stars in the sky, I felt compelled to pray to my Father in a special way. There is much I need to learn, and even more I want to know, in order to serve Him and fulfill His will for my life." And as Jesus closed his eyes, he said simply, "Father, not my will but thine be done. Amen."

Jesus had tugged at Mary's heartstrings as she witnessed him praying to the Father.

"God will reveal Himself to you, my son, and when the time is right, you will know all that you need know to handle any situation. Of this I am confident." Mary rose and kissed Jesus on the forehead. When she touched him, she felt renewed and refreshed with all the tranquility she had ever experienced.

"I am going downstairs to check on the other children. Let me know if you need me."

"I will always need you," Jesus replied, in the boyish voice she had not heard in many years. "God bless you, Mother."

Mary reentered the stillness of the downstairs, checked on her other children, and went back to bed. She thought about this experience with her son, along with all the loving thoughts and concerns she kept hidden in her heart. But tonight, Mary could not shake the sense of foreboding peril she had felt up on the roof. When she heard Jesus pray for God's will, she felt herself trembling. While she wanted the will of God to come to fruition in her son's life, she feared the consequences that might hold. From her understanding of prophecy, the coming Messiah was predicted to be a warrior that would lead God's army to liberation. *Could that really be her son?*

Kneeling beside her own bed, Mary prayed that God would strengthen her and protect Jesus against all the evil in the world. And, as she had heard her son say, she repeated, "Not my will, Lord, but thy will be done. Amen."

On the rooftop Jesus continued to pray to God, arms outstretched. He prayed for his family and for his own enlightenment. Jesus praised God for the beauty of the earth, for the stars in the heavens and for allowing him to experience the world through the eyes and body of a man.

Jennifer Taylor Wojcik
Philip G. Lilly D.Min.

Sitting once again, a shooting star zipped across the sky like an arrow shot from a taut bow. And as Jesus turned and faced the horizon, he recognized the star called Saturn; he knew it as the star that was believed to favor the Jews.

Looking in another direction, Jesus saw the moon was full and knew this was a sign of the approaching holiday Sukkoth, known as The Feast of the Tabernacles or Booths. This was a time to thank God for His provisions.

As Jesus bowed his head in reverence to God, he briefly caught a glimpse of himself back in a lowly manger, surrounded by Joseph and Mary. He felt the presence of angels, kings, and newly mowed hay and envisioned that same star. Then within a pure ephemeral moment, Jesus heard the words recorded in Zechariah:

> *Lo, your king comes to you; triumphant and victorious is he, humble and riding on a donkey, on a colt, the foal of a donkey* (Zechariah 9:9 NRSV).

He had ridden on the back of a donkey on the return trip from Egypt. He recognized these words as prophecy. As he had asked the Father through prayer, Jesus was growing in stature and in the knowledge of who he would become. He felt led by God's spirit to take the journey he had envisioned. And as a result of answered prayer, Jesus would ready himself for the trip.

XIX

Iri's Second Encounter with Jesus

When Jesus was age twenty-one, he spent a great deal of time at the local syna-gogue in Nazareth. There he would spend countless hours talking with the holy men as well as the most respected Israeli scholars, seeking to further his educa-tion and have his questions answered.

As a result, Jesus spent virtually every waking moment with these religious leaders, amazing them with his vast knowledge and challenging them with his thought-provoking questions. Always amazed at the depth of understanding and knowledge one so young exhibited, the elders allowed Jesus to follow them to the various classrooms, hearing again the recitations of the Law and prophets and assisting the younger Jewish boys who were struggling to memorize or recite what they were taught.

Jesus was, for all intents and purposes, serving as a student teacher. Rabbi Moshe sanctioned his interaction with the younger students, recognizing that no one knew the Jewish faith and Law any better than Jesus. Rabbi Moshe described him as "inspired."

Because Jesus was so busy with studying and teaching, he was not always available to work with Joseph in the carpentry shop. That responsibility had been given to Simon, who was six years younger than Jesus. While Simon attended classes at the synagogue, he was equally involved with learning his father's business.

One day Jesus decided that he would drop in on Joseph and Simon, so upon leaving the synagogue, he walked to the carpentry shop. As he approached, he heard a voice that was familiar and walked in to find it was Iri—the olive grower he had helped along the roadside a few years back.

Jesus overheard Iri relating the story of how Jesus had gone out of his way to assist him. Iri was sharing the story with both Joseph and Simon, making the comparison that Jesus had been just a lad—probably about the same age as Simon when they met.

As Jesus entered the carpentry shop, he heard Iri say, "And how is Jesus? Does he live in the area?"

Joseph smiled and said, "He is right here; you can ask him for yourself."

Iri's face broke into a wide smile as Jesus approached him and, with arms outstretched, hugged him.

"You have become such a strong man, Jesus," said Iri. "I might not have recognized you had I seen you on the street!"

Jesus answered, "And you, Iri, have not changed at all. I am happy to see you and pleased that you are doing well. What brings you to Nazareth?"

"I actually came to purchase new wheels for my carts. Your father, Joseph, was highly recommended, and it gave me the opportunity to share my business with your family business. I have never forgotten how kind you were to help me. I am not sure anyone else would have done all that you did," Iri said.

Jesus smiled at his friend Iri and said, "It seems that I was in the right place at the right time, Iri. And I am happy that Father's craftsmanship can help you in your business. He does make the finest wheels in all of northern Israel."

Joseph related the story of Jesus learning to craft a wheel and his run-in with the awl. "Jesus was a good student, but my teaching needed to include a bit more about being precise and careful with sharp objects! He still has a scar on his hand that shows his suffering in learning how to make a wheel."

Iri looked at the palm of Jesus's hand and shook his head. When he looked into Jesus's face, there was a brief moment between the two of them that could not accurately be described. It was as if Iri could see beyond the scar—to a new and more graphic wound. Iri trembled slightly and clasped the hand of Jesus, bringing it up to his cheek and kissing it.

Simon broke the silence of the moment, asking Joseph if he too could be taught to make a wheel.

Joseph nodded to Simon and simply said, "In due time, my son."

Iri finalized his order for wheels. As he turned to leave, he offered a handshake to both Joseph and Simon. When he turned to Jesus, he wrapped his arms around him and kissed his cheek. "Be safe, my friend. God be with you."

"May God be with you as well, Iri, until we will meet again."

XX

New Shoes and the Good News

He charged them to take nothing for their journey except a walking stick—no bread, no wallet for a collection bag, no money in their belts, but to go with sandals on their feet and not to put on two tunics (Mark 6:8–9 AMP).

Some years later, in Jesus's twenty-fourth year of life, he traveled to Rome. Though the trip was exhausting and taxing even for a young man, Jesus absorbed the beauty and culture as he toured the countryside along the road to Rome.

Having traveled a great distance, Jesus neared Tarsus, home of a philosophical school influenced by the Greek doctrines. Tarsus stood at the confluence of east and west, home to Greeks and Romans alike.

As Jesus approached the city, he noticed a sign over a door that read: House of Tanners. In those days, a tanner was a catch-all phrase for tentmakers and leatherworkers, as tents were originally made from goat skins that were sewn together.

Jesus's sandals were tattered and worn, and he needed to replace them. Here, at a house of tanners, he knew he could do just that.

Jesus knocked on the door. When the door opened, there stood Saul—the boy he had first met in the synagogue's school in Jerusalem.

Asking Jesus why he was in Tarsus, Saul appeared to be a bit uncomfortable in Jesus's presence. As Jesus explained his pilgrimage through Rome as one of furthering his education, Saul asked where he was staying.

Jesus responded that he would be looking for an inn but that he was in need of new sandals to continue his journey. Saul explained that the owners of the home were husband-and-wife tentmakers named Aquila and Priscilla and that he had taken up temporary residence with them.

Jesus asked Saul what he was doing in Tarsus, to which Saul replied that he had become a tentmaker as well as a teacher.

"As you may remember, it has long been my desire to teach others," Saul said.

"And I recall you were an excellent student in Jerusalem and not one to be embarrassed by your own depth of knowledge," Jesus replied.

"Yes, I worked hard to learn all that I could about the Law and prophets as well as Jewish customs, and now I take that message to other Jews so that their lives will follow the correct path."

"Yet you are a tentmaker, Saul. That craft must be tedious," Jesus said.

"And you, Jesus, are you still a carpenter?" Saul asked.

"Yes, my father taught me well. He also taught my brothers James, Joses, Judah, and Simon," Jesus replied.

After a moment of awkward silence, Jesus inquired again about sandals.

Saul said, "I am sure that Aquila has sandals to your liking and size. He and his wife should be here soon. In the meantime, may I offer you water or something to eat?"

Jesus answered, "Water would be most welcomed, Saul."

Just as Saul returned with the cup of water, Aquila and Priscilla entered their home.

Saul said, "This is Jesus of Nazareth. He and I attended school at the synagogue in Jerusalem some years ago. He is traveling to Rome and in need of new sandals."

Aquila said, "Jesus of Nazareth, welcome to our humble home. I will ask Priscilla to bring sandals in so you can select those you like best." He nodded to Priscilla, who made her way to another room to fetch the shoes.

"So, Jesus," said Aquila, "do you also teach as Saul teaches?"

"I am quickly approaching that time in my life," said Jesus "I will no doubt be teaching many things to many people, but now is not my appointed time to do so. That time draws near, and I look ahead with eagerness and great anticipation."

A look of puzzlement ran across Saul's face, but before he could question Jesus, Priscilla entered the room with sandals and laid them at Jesus's feet.

"These should do nicely," said Jesus as he slipped the new sandals onto his feet. "They are well made and fit me perfectly. If you will tell me the cost, I will pay you."

Aquila quoted Jesus a price, and as Jesus paid him, he asked where Jesus was spending the night. When Jesus told him he had yet to find an inn, Aquila offered their rooftop for the night at no cost.

Jesus graciously accepted Aquila's offer, picked up his worn sandals, and wearing the new ones, went up to the rooftop to rest.

When Priscilla had prepared the evening meal, she walked up the stairway to call Jesus to share their supper. There she found Jesus quietly praying on his knees. Sensing her presence, Jesus turned to her saying, "Yes?"

"Please join us for the evening meal, sir," Priscilla offered.

Jesus was seated next to Saul. They gave thanks for the meal and ate until they were full.

When they had finished eating, Jesus lifted a cup of wine and said, "Father, bless this cup and all who are here." Then, turning to his dinner companions, he said, "Please share in this cup of salvation." Aquila, Priscilla, and Saul then drank from the cup Jesus had offered them and resumed their conversation.

Saul asked, "So, Jesus, what did you mean about teaching? You said it was not your appointed time to teach. What do you mean by that?"

"As you know, Saul, a good teacher must learn everything he can so that his words have meaning for the students. I am learning every minute of every day and will take my teachings to the earth's farthest reaches at the proper time and in the appropriate place."

"And do you plan to teach in a synagogue or university?" Saul asked.

"I will be a traveling teacher and will be assisted by some of my closest friends in educating others about the *good news*."

"Good news?" Saul scoffed. "I dare say the time has *not* come for you to spread good news. The world as we know it is becoming divided, with kings fighting kings and man fighting man for what they want. I see very little good news in the offing."

"Then it is not your time to hear the good news, Saul, but there will come a time when your eyes will be opened to the truth that the good news brings."

"Your words leave me with only questions, Jesus," Saul said as he shook his head. "But then you have always looked for hidden meanings in everything. Perhaps you are a philosopher rather than a teacher?"

"I am who I am. And you will see me with new eyes at the allotted time, and then my message will be clear to you," Jesus answered.

Rising from the supper table, Jesus kindly thanked Aquila and Priscilla for their hospitality, for comfortable lodging, and for his new sandals.

The next morning, Jesus left the tanners' house just past dawn. Saul would not encounter Jesus again until they would ultimately meet on the road to Damascus.

XXI

Jesus in Hindustan

It was a rainy late-November day when Mary was awakened by sounds coming from the bedroom adjacent to her own room. She rolled out of bed slowly, ambling toward the door. Peering out the doorway, she could see in the early dawn that it was Jesus, carrying a light travel pack.

"Where are you going, my son?" Mary asked.

"It is time for me to travel eastward and meet with our brothers and sisters," he replied. Jesus was now twenty-three.

Mary, a bit perplexed, dressed quickly and met Jesus in the main living area just as he was about to exit the front door.

She asked again, "But where are you going, my son?"

Jesus responded, "As you know, many in our family were exiled or fled as the nation fell into disarray. I feel led to travel to Hindustan to meet them and welcome them back into the family fold." Jesus was of course referring to the time in Israel's history when Nebuchadnezzar II, King of Babylon, had taken over the southern kingdom of Judah. Many Jews had either been forcibly exiled or had fled to Egypt and areas east of the Indus River.

To Mary, it seemed like an odd time of the year to start out on a long journey to Pakistan and India. But Mary had long since learned to accept the choices that Jesus made; he was independent and wise for his age.

Mary's motherly instincts had taken over. "What will you eat? Where will you find shelter?"

"*Jehovah jireh*," was Jesus's response; "God will provide." And with that, he kissed his mother on the forehead and slipped out the door.

Mary's heart sank. She had come to depend on the quiet yet confident strength of her son Jesus.

Traveling from his hometown of Nazareth to Hindustan would take Jesus months to accomplish. He had packed two extra pairs of sandals into his bag, indicative of the amount of walking he knew would be involved in this journey.

He would first be traveling north to Damascus —the easiest leg of his journey—having well-traveled roads through numerous small towns and villages. As a traveling rabbi, he could count on open doors and meals.

Once on the main road north leading out of Nazareth, Jesus met some Jewish merchants carrying a variety of goods to a large marketplace in Damascus. They were traveling with their families. The leader and chief merchant of the group was a well-established Jerusalem tradesman named Adnah. He was a dealer in high-end pottery used for cooking.

Seeing that Jesus was a rabbi, Adnah offered him transportation on one of their carts in exchange for tutoring his children on the journey to Damascus. The children, all female, ranged in age from three to nine and were receptive to having a tutor teach them the Law. When Jesus was introduced to the children, they immediately liked him.

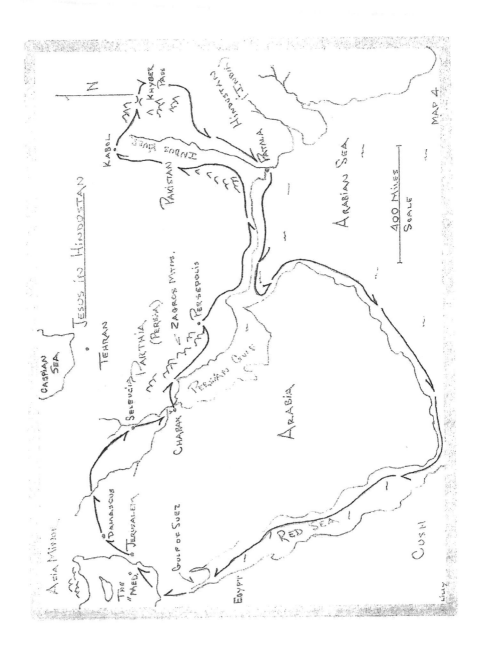

Nazareth to Damascus would take nearly a full week to complete, as the journey was eighty-one miles. For the children under Jesus's care, it was a fun experience, learning and laughing under the tutelage of this young rabbi, Jesus. Deborah, the oldest daughter, took the lead in greeting Jesus and had offered him a seat in the cart.

During the trip, Jesus taught them a full range of subjects, including language arts, science, geography, and the Law of Moses. During evenings together, the parents joined the sessions and participated by asking a flurry of questions.

Several miles outside of Damascus, the caravan was stopped at a checkpoint controlled by the local Roman military. The military served as customs officers and inspected and questioned them about their reasons for traveling.

The Roman commander demanded the standard road tariff in order to "give Caesar what is Caesar's" and avoid arrest.

The full caravan passed through the city gates and headed to the central city market. Once inside the city, Jesus asked that the cart stop so he could gather his personal items and be on his way.

As he did so, Adnah approached Jesus and asked if he would consider becoming the children's permanent tutor. Jesus graciously declined, saying that he would only be in Damascus for a short period before traveling on to Hindustan. Adnah nodded, smiled, and gave Jesus a pouch of money as extra thanks for his service. Jesus turned to Adnah, smiled, and waved good-bye to the young ladies, saying simply, "Shalom."

And Jesus returned to Galilee in the power of the Spirit, and news about Him spread through all the surrounding district, And He began teaching in their synagogues and was praised by all (Luke 4:14 NASB).

Jennifer Taylor Wojcik
Philip G. Lilly D.Min.

Damascus was one of the largest cities in the region. There Jesus found adequate places to lodge and opportunities to receive compensation for teaching and tutoring.

Without difficulty, Jesus found shelter in a hostel intended for travelers and short-term residents. Settling in Damascus, Jesus quickly became known for his intellect and teaching ability. And, having mastered multiple languages, Jesus was asked by local officials to translate documents and assist foreign visitors with trade and/or legal issues.

A Roman proconsul had arrived in the city to negotiate new trade routes between Tehran and Damascus. Local officials, aware of Jesus's skills as a righteous arbiter and linguist, sent a messenger to ask that Jesus participate in the negotiations.

The messenger found Jesus at his hostel, reading and discussing Jewish scrolls with several local rabbis as well as a philosopher. The messenger relayed the request from the proconsul and was notably shaken when Jesus did not end his meeting with the rabbis. Instead, Jesus said he would happily see the proconsul shortly after midday, giving time to conclude this meeting.

The government house was located in the center of Damascus. It was constructed as a separate and distinct "walled city" within Damascus proper. Guards at the main gate had been informed that Jesus would be coming. As promised, Jesus arrived at the government house shortly after noon. The guards, with spears tightly gripped by their sides, motioned him through the gates.

Jesus was led to a finely appointed meeting room filled with officials representing Caesar, the local Damascus government, and an entourage of dignitaries who were seeking new trade routes.

Reflecting their status as high-ranking officials, the meeting participants were opulently dressed. Jesus was dressed in a very simple full-length tunic, covered by a light brown cloak, and his head was adorned by a simple skull cap with a piece of material folded into a band around the turned-up edge, giving the appearance of a modest turban.

Needless to say, Jesus stood out by both his appearance and mode of dress. When he walked into the room, all eyes turned to him as they immediately recognized Jesus as a Jew. There was a moment of quiet but implicit tension. Jesus scanned the room, lowered his eyes in respect, and then simply nodded, breaking the tension.

As the meeting progressed, Jesus noted there were two sticking points. The first revolved around the cost of securing the routes and the prorated cost which would be passed on to the users. The second involved the attitude of the mayor of Damascus—a physically large man with an ego that matched his size. It was clear to Jesus that the mayor's intention was to run the meeting, directing all outcomes in his favor.

Jesus sensed that the majority of the participants were becoming frustrated with the mayor and his bullying tactics. At a critical point in the meeting, Jesus spoke in Aramaic, quoting Proverbs 11:3–4 (NASB): "When pride comes, then comes dishonor, but with the humble is wisdom. The integrity of the upright will guide them, but the falseness of the treacherous will destroy them."

He then translated the Proverb into Latin, and afterward there was a moment of silence. As the meeting resumed, the mayor was noticeably quiet. Looking directly into the eyes of Jesus, the proconsul from Tehran smiled, indicating his approval with a simple nod.

An hour or so later, the meeting concluded with an agreement, handshakes, and bows. As Jesus departed, Proconsul Aelius stopped him and personally thanked him for his assistance. The proconsul started to turn away when he paused and, turning back to Jesus, said, "If there is anything I can do for you, or if you ever come to Seleucia, please allow me to assist you."

Jesus smiled and replied, "I had planned to leave tomorrow for points east."

Aelius responded, "Then you must come as part of my company, and we can talk along the way." Looking down at Jesus's worn sandals, he continued. "You can save those sandals for another journey."

Early the next morning, Jesus met the proconsul and his contingent outside the city government center. Escorting them was a detachment of Roman frontier soldiers that would accompany the group back to Seleucia.

ღ

From Damascus, the group traveled east via the Silk Road through desolate and arid regions in the Upper Mesopotamian area, which encompassed Northern Syria and Iraq. Though desolate, the route was well traveled. It was frequented by merchants moving back and forth between China and cities in the Mediterranean rim.

Precious metals, glass, and dyed fabrics moved east on camels and carts to India and China. Silk, spices, and rice moved back to the west to both Damascus and Rome. Merchants and travelers could be found on carts, donkeys, camels, and various other hoofed animals.

Over a period of several weeks, the group slowly moved along well-traveled gravel and stone roads. Along the route and at the end of the day, Aelius and Jesus discussed philosophy, mathematics, astronomy, and religion. Aelius was astounded by the depth and breadth of Jesus's education and understanding of the world and beyond. His own education had been formally planned and executed at the most prestigious schools in Rome, and now he was learning from a humble Jew that spoke more languages than he.

And all who heard Him were amazed at His understanding and His answers
(Luke 2:47 NASB).

Eventually the troop reached the Euphrates River. The river was far too wide to engineer a usable bridge. Locals instead provided several locations where small barges could be pulled across the river with hemp rope. The fee at most locations ranged from three to five denarii, depending on the time of year and volume of traffic.

Due to the official status of the proconsul's group, there was no fee for their barge. One could literally feel the anger and tension as the group cut to the front of the waiting line and stated their official status to avoid the charge. No one was happy—neither the local travelers nor those pulling the barge.

As the first part of the group began loading onto the barge, one of the workers made a disparaging remark to one of the Roman soldiers. Quickly the soldier barked back at the barge worker, unsheathed his sword, and moved to cut the worker's hand off. Jesus stepped between the two and began speaking in

Latin to the soldier. The soldier lowered his sword and nodded to Jesus. Jesus then turned to the barge worker and seemed to be admonishing him in his native Persian language. Thanks to the intervention of Jesus, a struggle was averted, and all within hearing distance were amazed at what Jesus had just accomplished.

A large group of locals gathered on the east bank to observe the rare occurrence of a high-ranking Roman official crossing the river.

Some two hours later, their route across the river was completed, and the Roman contingent traveled on to Seleucia and to the proconsul's office.

The proconsul was welcomed back by his household and staff. He had been gone for several months. During his absence, various decisions and issues had been placed in a holding status awaiting his return. Once settled in, Aelius asked that Jesus join him in the main hall of the central administrative complex.

There Jesus and Aelius discussed a variety of municipal and societal issues now pending. As Aelius had come to learn, Jesus's approach to each issue was typically unconventional and yet creative and insightful.

ೕ ೆ ೂ ೨ ೦

During a future consultation, Aelius abruptly changed the direction of their conversation and said to Jesus, "I know that you had planned to travel east to Hindustan and beyond to reunite with relatives, but I would like you to consider becoming chief of staff in my administration. You would be a great asset to me, not to mention the large community of Jews living here."

Jesus was well aware of the large community of Jews and had been meeting with many of them during his brief stay. Word had spread quickly throughout the Jewish community that a visiting rabbi was available for study, prayer, and consultation. Jesus had also met with a group of rabbis and provided them with lessons from the ancient writings.

Jesus paused for a moment and then looked directly into the eyes of Aelius and answered, "A man that does not follow his calling is like a bird that does not build a nest. I must leave soon, as my destiny is rapidly unfolding."

Aelius then asked, "When will you be leaving?"

"By tomorrow's first light," Jesus responded. "I must leave now to prepare." He then left and went to his quarters.

Early the next morning, Jesus was awakened by a captain of the local Roman guardsmen named Artimus. "Sir, I have come to wake and ready you for your journey."

Artimus had in fact been sent along with a small contingent of soldiers to accompany Jesus on his journey. That trek would take Jesus and the soldiers to the boundary of the Roman Empire, where the Persian Empire began.

Jesus was already packed and ready to begin the journey. He was pleased to know that Proconsul Aelius had approved security and company for this next leg of his journey.

Just outside his quarters, Jesus discovered that his traveling group included ten crack Roman soldiers, two wagons with supplies, and a personal assistant for Jesus. At first Jesus refused the assistant but was quickly convinced that this was the express wish of the proconsul. Jesus then graciously agreed, and the group departed Seleucia before the sun rose.

To expedite the trip south, two large river barges had been procured by the soldiers at the direction of the proconsul. The timing was perfect, as the barges would also be carrying military goods south on the Tigris River to the Roman military outpost at Charax.

As the journey began, the Roman officer leading the group made it clear to Jesus that their escort of him would end in Charax. Once outside the Meshan District, the safety of Jesus could no longer be guaranteed by the Romans. He would be on his own for the remainder of his journey to Hindustan.

The traveling distance between Seleucia and Charax was approximately three hundred miles and would take at least a month.

For this reason we must pay much closer attention to what we have heard, lest we drift away from it (Hebrews 2:1 NASB).

Jennifer Taylor Wojcik
Philip G. Lilly D.Min.

As the barges slowly made their way down the winding Tigris, it seemed they were hardly moving at all. At times the river looked like a large coiled snake moving through a grassy marsh. Glancing up occasionally, those aboard noticed that they had quietly moved another measure downstream. At the end of each day's journey, the pilot looked for a clearing on the bank of the river where they could safely tie up for the night. Fortunately, on this trip a waxing full moon provided the opportunity to travel after nightfall and prior to daybreak. Jesus spent most of his time aboard the barge praying. He would find a quiet spot on the boat, cross his legs, and lift his hands toward the heavens. The soldiers, as well as the barge crew, respected his time and space and did not interrupt. On one occasion after Jesus's prayer time, a Roman soldier named Pamphillius asked Jesus what god he was praying to for such long periods of time.

Jesus responded, "The only one God, our Father in heaven, who created and sustains all that you see."

Pamphillius replied, "Teacher, is not Caesar a god?"

Jesus's short answer was "Give respect to your leaders and most to Caesar, but in God there is salvation for all who acknowledge Him."

Several days passed, and the barges finally arrived in Charax. It was a mid-day landing on a Monday in January. The barges were quickly off-loaded by local laborers.

Jesus did not remain for the unloading to be completed. He quickly gathered his belongings as well as some rations and thanked the commander of the Roman soldiers. As Jesus walked off the dock, he heard someone yell out, "Rabbi, Rabbi, please." It was Pamphillius, the Roman soldier who had spoken to him earlier. Jesus stopped and walked back and met the soldier.

Pamphillius reached out his hands, palms up, and said, "Please bless me, my Lord."

Jesus peered into the soldier's eyes and said, "Bless you, my son. May you come to know the truth of the one and only true God, and may He dwell in you forever."

Two years later, Pamphillius would be promoted and transferred to the legion garrison in Jerusalem.

When the centurion, who was standing right in front of Him, saw the way He breathed His last, he said, "Truly this man was the Son of God! (Mark 15:39 NASB).

O God, You are my God; I shall seek You earnestly; My soul thirsts for You, my flesh yearns for You, In a dry and weary land where there is no water. Thus I have seen You in the sanctuary, To see Your power and Your glory. Because Your loving-kindness is better than life, My lips will praise You. So I will bless You as long as I live; I will lift up my hands in Your name. My soul is satisfied as with marrow and fatness, And my mouth offers praises with joyful lips. When I remember You on my bed, I meditate on You in the night watches, For You have been my help, And in the shadow of Your wings I sing for joy. My soul clings to You; Your right hand upholds me. But those who seek my life to destroy it, Will go into the depths of the earth. They will be delivered over to the power of the sword; They will be a prey for foxes. But the king will rejoice I God; Everyone who swears by Him will glory, For the mouths of those who speak lies will be stopped (Psalm 63:1–11 NASB).

Wasting no time, Jesus traveled east out of Charax into the Zagros Mountains, where he found the Royal Road heading southeast. The Royal Road was an expansive byway, mountainous and rugged and built under the rule of Darius I. From that junction Jesus traveled on foot to Persepolis and then on to Harmozeia, on the Arabian Sea.

Information concerning this final leg of Jesus's journey to Hindustan seems to have been lost in antiquity. Yet fragments of writing discovered in the region point to the possibility that within two months, Jesus arrived in Hindustan and the city of Regio Patalis.

There you will serve gods, the work of man's hands, wood and stone, which neither see nor hear nor eat nor smell (Deuteronomy 4:28 NASB).

Months passed as Jesus met and talked with distant relatives and locals in Regio Patalis and other areas in that region.

Based on physical appearance alone, there were distinct similarities between Jesus and the locals. Many of the elders still spoke in broken Hebrew—an indicator of ancestral connections. Yet Jesus noted that these people had abandoned their ancient worship of the one true God, choosing now to worship idols, Buddha, or nothing at all. The influence of Hinduism and Buddhism was dominant throughout the whole community of Jews as well as other residents. Jesus found them to be a sad lot, yet they were seemingly content.

It had been several months since Jesus had left Nazareth. He began to long for the fellowship of his family as well as his mother's cooking. The Spirit led Jesus to make preparations to depart for home.

The journey home began dockside in Patalis, where Jesus had earlier met Singh Khan. Singh was the seasoned captain of a one-hundred-foot merchant ship powered by sails and supported by competent oarsmen when needed. The ship would be traveling over the southern-ocean leg of the Silk Road.

The ship had been loaded with exotic wood, locally woven goods, precious gems, and large jars of linseed oil. All these goods were bound for a port located at the northern end of the Gulf of Suez. From there the goods would be transported over land where they would then be loaded onto another ship in Alexandria. Their ultimate destination was Rome. While carrying all these expensive items, their most precious cargo was Jesus. It was the final leg of his journey back to Nazareth.

The time of Passover was nearing on this early April morning when Mary heard a knock on her door. She opened it to find her son Jesus, now sporting a full beard and wearing tattered, well-worn sandals. Almost in disbelief Mary said, "What day is it?"

"It is Yom Shish," said Jesus, meaning the sixth day. "Tomorrow, we rest and worship. Then I will tell you of my journey as well as the journey ahead."

Jesus smiled, taking his mother's hand, and kissed her on the forehead as he had done many times before. Mary buried her head in his chest and cried tears of joy. Her son was home, at least for now.

XXII

The Death of Joseph the Carpenter

But the people who trust the Lord will become strong again. They will rise up as an eagle in the sky; they will run and not need rest; they will walk and not become tired (Isaiah 40:31 NIV).

Jews were promised health if they obeyed God's laws and were given a number of laws about health. Physician's services were considered "suspect" by the Jewish people, who believed that illnesses were a result of some sinful act—a punishment of sorts. The correct procedure in illness was regarded to be prayer to God.

Typically, sickness was not linked to food or drink but attributed to the will and judgment of God. The people believed that prayer was more effective than medicine. But in those days under Roman rule, every village was required by law to have a physician. Disease was a major problem due to poor sanitation and pollution. Diseases such as dysentery, cholera, typhoid, blindness, and deafness (often caused by the arid climate and blowing sand) were accompanied by crippling diseases. Epilepsy and nervous disorders were common as well.

Practicing in the village of Nazareth was a Greek physician named Jayson who had become a doctor after completing his training at the medical school in Alexandria, Egypt. Jayson was well respected by the Roman government and had been placed in Nazareth by the local Roman administrator.

Having completed his travel through Rome and Hindustan, Jesus had matured greatly. When Jesus came to visit his parents in Nazareth, he expected little more than spending some quality time with his brothers and sisters and their spouses, enjoying Yom Shish, and helping Mary and Joseph with whatever he could. Upon his return, he learned that his father was not well.

As soon as Jesus saw the face of Joseph, he kneeled by his bedside and prayed. After his prayer, Jesus sought out Mary, asking her to share with him what she knew of Joseph's illness. Mary told Jesus that he had been ailing for a time, and that with each passing day, Joseph appeared to grow weaker.

Mary described Joseph's symptoms and somewhat reluctantly shared with Jesus what the local physician had said. Mary told Jesus she was concerned that the baseline cause of Joseph's progressing illness was due to a sin he had committed. But Jesus turned to his mother, kindly telling her that he believed Joseph's condition was so that the works of God might be revealed through him.

Jayson, the physician, diagnosed Joseph with having dysentery; a common disease of the lower intestine caused by parasites or bacteria and marked by inflammation and diarrhea. The impurities found in virtually all sources of water made this a particularly widespread health concern.

Joseph had a high spiking fever, and then hours of chills that Mary could not warm him from. Mary had stayed by his side, swabbing his brow with cool cloths, and warming him with blankets as best she could.

Joseph was now bedridden, and Mary had prayed that he would see Jesus before he passed. When Jesus arrived, Mary thanked God for answering her prayers. She secretly believed that their son would prevent Joseph's death, but Jesus had not yet come to the appointed time to perform these miracles.

"My son," Mary said to Jesus, "your father is gravely ill. He would be so pleased to know that you are at his bedside praying for him."

"My Father has been at work through this very day, and He will continue to work through his servant Joseph. Joseph has been a wonderful father and has taught me many things. Would that I could make him well, but his fate is in the hands of our Father in heaven," said Jesus.

He bowed his head and prayed aloud, "Father, if it is in your divine plan to leave this honorable man in our midst, we praise you. But if your will is for Joseph to be with you in your kingdom, we ask that his path be lightened and his journey hastened. Mary and I ask only that your will be done. Amen."

Jennifer Taylor Wojcik
Philip G. Lilly D.Min.

Within a matter of minutes, Joseph opened his eyes slowly and smiled at both his wife and Jesus. Looking up at his once youthful son, Joseph recognized Jesus's maturity and strength as a man. With all assurance of his future, the beloved carpenter and father then went to be with his ancestors. The man who had lived his life trusting that God was directing his actions was now in the midst of his creator and Lord.

XXIII

Family Affairs

Jesus's siblings included James, Joses, Judah, Simon, Miriam, Assia, and Lydia, plus their spouses. To fulfill the Law of the Jews, Jesus as the eldest was to now assist his mother in restructuring the family and solidifying their relationships. But first, Jesus had to make all the arrangements for Joseph's burial.

Since Joseph had died, there was much to do. There were arrangements to be made: a burial place had to be secured; the local rabbi had to be contacted to officiate at the funeral service, and there were specific Jewish rites that had to be performed.

It was incumbent upon Jesus to secure a burial place as quickly as possible as well as name the "guards" or *shomerim* of the body, who would stay with Joseph until the burial. The burial, by Jewish law, had to take place quickly, due in part to the hot climate, which led to rapid decomposition. However, burials were forbidden on a Sabbath or a holy day.

Upon death, the shomerim would wash the body of the deceased, close the eyes, and dress the body in a simple linen shroud. They would then light candles on the floor surrounding the body. As a sign of respect, the body was covered with blankets and never left alone.

Jesus had to locate a cave to house his earthly father's remains, and in these times, a natural cave often sheltered several bodies that had been laid to rest. A stone would be rolled in front of the cave's opening, and the cave's exterior wall would be painted white as a warning to the living that the dead were entombed there.

Jennifer Taylor Wojcik
Philip G. Lilly D.Min.

When the burial day came, the house of Joseph was a somber one. Friends and relatives gathered together at the burial site. Afterward, the extended family and the immediate family (including spouses of Jesus's siblings) gathered at Joseph's modest home, where they shared a traditional Jewish meal. The "meal of condolence" consisted of eggs, which symbolized life, and bread that had been prepared by Joseph's sister-in-law, Ruth.

It was now evening, and the daughters of Joseph, as well as Mary, were working to clean up after the meal. The extended family had departed, leaving only the immediate family at home. It was eerily quiet, and the ladies were going about their chores as expected. In the next room, Mary heard the sons of Joseph having an intense conversation about their relationships to one another.

Mary overheard her son Judah asking, "Jesus, are you in charge of the family now?"

Before Jesus could answer, Joses said, "Why? You're not really our *brother*, are you?"

Jesus responded by saying, "You have rightly asked these questions. As Joseph's oldest son, it is my responsibility to make all the arrangements for a proper burial, so in that respect, I am in charge of the family for now."

Jesus approached Joses and said, "I *am* your brother, but by all accounts I am your *half brother*. Let me explain this so that you hear it from me and understand. Mary is the birth mother to all of us, but *my* birth was the result of the Holy Spirit of God selecting Mary to become pregnant and bring me into the world. Each of the rest of you were as a result of the coupling of Mary and Joseph, our earthly parents.

Mary walked into the room. "My children, you are the offspring of Joseph, and Joseph was chosen by God to be the earthly father of Jesus. He was indeed father to all of you. Your father and I were chosen to raise and nurture the Son of God, and you are blessed to have him as your half brother. Simon—you are the youngest son. Do you understand?" Mary asked.

Simon boldly rose to his feet. "Yes, Jesus is my brother."

With that proclamation, the siblings returned to their previous activities, the ladies to the kitchen and the young men to their own banter. Mary walked again to the doorway to make sure the conversation had progressed, when she heard raucous laughter from the sons of Joseph.

Aghast that frivolity had taken over her home on this somber occasion, Mary feverously entered the room. "Jesus," said Mary, "you of all my sons should know better than to act like this. You know the first seven days following your father's death are to be spent in intense mourning, so why would you laugh and joke at a time like this?"

"Mother," Jesus said as he approached her. "We are thinking and speaking of Joseph in the most respectful way. You must hear the story that James just told us about Judah and Joseph. We are honoring him *privately*—by remembering the great times we had with him."

Then looking at James, Jesus asked him to relate the story for their mother and their sisters.

James meekly started his story. "We were in the marketplace together, just outside father's carpentry shop, and we noticed some young women making their way toward us. Judah was so mesmerized with watching them that he did not notice me tying his tunic sash to a nail on the wall outside the shop. As the women came closer, I yelled out to Judah and told him Father was calling us. He dashed toward the door of the shop and was left wearing nothing more than his undergarments. The girls giggled and laughed and pointed at Judah. It was so funny."

Judah said, "Yeah, it was funny then, but what we didn't know is that Father had watched from the window and witnessed everything that happened. When he did call us to the shop, he said, 'James, I saw what you did. Get over here and sit down on this stool; I want to talk to you and your brothers about what just happened.' When James sat on the stool, the legs fell off it, and James ended up on the ground. Father had rigged the stool's legs so that would happen." Judah was laughing aloud as were the other siblings.

Jesus said, "Father was teaching us a lesson."

James said, "Yeah, it was one of those lessons about treating people the way you'd like to be treated."

Judah said, "Father was wise and knew how to get his point across. And besides, you never know *who* is watching."

Jesus turned to Mary. "You see, Mother? There is respect in sharing fond memories of those who have passed on. We meant no harm or disrespect in remembering good times with Joseph. It is with love and respect that we honor him in this way."

"I suppose," said Mary, "but keep your sharing of funny stories inside our home—at least for the next thirty days...Rabbi Moshe would be horrified." Quietly Mary reentered the kitchen area, with a slight smile on her face.

The ladies reconvened in the kitchen area to finish their chores. When they saw the look on Mary's face, they quietly began sharing some of their most loved memories of their father. Mary made no comment but was inwardly pleased that all the children loved and respected their father. In the days to come, Mary would have stories of her own to share with all of them.

XXIV

Jesus as Head of the Family

In this era, a woman who survived her husband was thrust into a precarious state. She could not inherit from her husband, but she could remain in her husband's family *if* the next of kin would take her in marriage. More often than not, the widow was without financial support, so the Law stated that widows were to be protected.

Once the declared thirty days of intense mourning ended, Mary approached Jesus to seek his counsel and pose a question.

"Jesus, what am I to do now without a proper husband? I know the teachings and laws of our people, but there is not a brother of Joseph who is unmarried. What should I do to keep our law, serve God and continue to care for our family?"

Jesus said, "We are all a part of God's family, and He will take care of his own. Whether married or single, we must live devoted to the Lord. I believe that because you are devoted to God, you should ask this question of Him through your prayers. You and the elders have taught me to believe that His will for your life will become clear through prayer, and once your prayer is answered, you can act accordingly."

Mary was quiet for a time, thinking on what Jesus had said to her. "My son, you have become full of wisdom and grown in your faith. I will pray about these things and ask for direction from God. I will also pray for Joseph's relatives."

"You should not worry about the relatives of Joseph. The family has always come to the aid and assistance of other relations, and any change would be unlikely. Think of the support and love we received when traveling to Egypt to escape the wrath of King Herod and then upon our return to Jerusalem.

Remember Joseph's uncle Hiram, who took him into his carpentry business, and as a result, Joseph made him prosperous and well respected throughout Egypt. Hiram's descendants look on you in great favor and will surely not abandon you now," Jesus said.

Mary smiled at her son as she said, "As Joseph's eldest son, you now bear a great weight of responsibility for me as well as your siblings. I would not want your future impeded because we are a yoke that weighs you down, but instead I pray for the way to be clear for all your heavenly Father has intended you to do."

"My heavenly Father has appointed me to complete His will, and so it will be. There is nothing on earth that will keep me from doing as He asks, and my mother, brothers, and sisters are *not* a burden," Jesus said. "I believe each of my siblings will gladly take on additional responsibilities to make family life all that it should be."

"We should call a family meeting to discuss these things. Will you preside over it so that everyone understands our needs?"

"Of course, Mother. I have already prayed about this," Jesus said.

Jesus spoke with each of his siblings individually. He approached James first, then Joses, Judah, and down the line to the youngest, Lydia. They would all meet after the evening meal, three days from then.

Mary spent much of the next three days in prayer. She prayed for Jesus and that her family would not become burdensome or interfere in the plans God had made for her eldest son. She asked for guidance in deciding what to do about remarriage. Mary prayed that her own desire to remain single be taken away if God willed otherwise. And she asked that God bring blessings on the other children in the family, who clearly now needed to contribute all they could to keep the family intact.

When the evening arrived, the discussion took place around the family table. Jesus spoke first, sharing their mother's concerns about following Jewish Law. Jesus shared Mary's desire to follow the Law but explained to his brothers and sisters that he had urged Mary to seek God's direction through prayer.

Mary stood in front of her children, saying, "I have prayed over the past three days, and I believe that the will of God is for me to remain as I am, a widow, without plans to remarry. Joseph's death occurred at a time when his brothers were all married, and that is a sign to me." Mary looked around the table for reactions, but received none. "Jesus reminded me that we are God's family, and we must believe He will care for us."

Jesus spoke then, saying, "As the eldest, it is expected that I am to be the head of the family. But just as our mother has done, I have prayed for guidance as well. As has clearly been shown to me, each of us must now step up and contribute our best efforts to insure the sanctity of the family."

James spoke. "Jesus, I am but two years your junior and am willing and able to help provide for our family. I have become a good carpenter and can reopen Joseph's shop as soon as we deem it appropriate to do so. I would be pleased and honored to follow in Joseph's footsteps."

Joses and Judah said they would help James in any way possible. Joses said he could handle the deliveries, and Judah offered to assist James to further learn the trade so that one day he could become his brother's partner.

Not to be outdone, Simon, who was now age nineteen, offered to handle the orders that came into the carpentry shop and substitute for any of his brothers who needed to be away. He also volunteered to clean their working quarters daily.

The sisters were all in agreement that they would accept all the responsibilities of the housework and cooking, plus they would assist Mary in cleaning their clothing and the daily trips to the marketplace for water and other supplies.

Mary looked up and down as her children sat around the table they had eaten their meals on for years. Mary had served them—all of them on this very spot, and now her children were planning just how they could serve her. She had a great sense of pride in her children and was thankful for their willingness to pull together as a family united.

"You see?" said Jesus. "God has provided all these hands and hearts to work together. We will trust in His will, knowing that our mother, Mary, is a woman of great favor."

XXV

John the Baptist

As John was completing his work, he said: "Who do you suppose I am? I am not the one you are looking for. But there is one coming after me whose sandals I am not worthy to untie" (Acts 13:25 NIV).

John—who subsequently became known as *John the Baptist*—and Jesus grew up separately, all the while being prepared for the time when their lives would intersect. John and Jesus were related through their mothers, Elizabeth and Mary, who were cousins.

John and Jesus were close in age. The Bible speaks of Mary's initial encounter with Elizabeth after each woman had conceived a child, saying that Elizabeth felt her child *leap within her womb* as she embraced Mary. Both women had experienced miracles from God: Elizabeth's conception in old age and Mary's pregnancy by Immaculate Conception.

John and Jesus were destined to meet, and John was intended to let others know that a messiah was coming. God told John that when the time came, he would recognize the Messiah.

Before the start of his public ministry, John stayed with his elderly parents, Zachariah and Elizabeth, in *Ein Karem*, a village near Jerusalem. At about age thirty, John moved to the Judean wilderness, living close to the Jordan River in order to fulfill his God-given mission. The Jordan River flows south, from the Sea of Galilee, to the Dead Sea and would ultimately serve John as the ideal place to immerse repentant sinners, recognizing them as believers of God.

Jennifer Taylor Wojcik
Philip G. Lilly D.Min.

John the Baptist would tell anyone who listened that he had come to prepare the way for the coming Messiah. To fulfill his directive from God, John attracted a continuous series of listeners as he delivered God's message.

The people knew about the prophecies and were watching out for God to come and visit and redeem His people. In that day, baptism meant that they had admitted their sins and were cleansing themselves of those sins via immersion in water. Many responded and wanted to be set free of their sins, and John proceeded to baptize them in the River Jordan.

Priests and Levites came to John, asking who he was. They feared that he was Elijah, or the prophet. John's testimony was that he was the one who baptized with water, that another—one who was greater than he—would come to baptize with the Holy Spirit.

At the same time, John began alerting the crowds that the Messiah would be appearing soon.

> *I baptize you with water to show that your hearts and lives have changed. But there is one coming after me who is greater than I am, whose sandals I am not good enough to carry. He will baptize you with the Holy Spirit and fire* (Matthew 3:11 NIV).

John came to be trusted as a messenger of God and clearly stated that the will of God would be carried out. As more and more people came forward for baptism, the numbers of believers grew exponentially. As those believers went out and shared the word, more came to John to be baptized and to hear him speak of the coming Messiah.

When Jesus was about age thirty, he recognized by the Holy Spirit's guidance that his time of teaching was at hand. He left Nazareth and headed toward the Jordan River, where John was baptizing people.

When John saw Jesus, he said, "Why do you come to me to be baptized? I need to be baptized by you!" (Matthew 3:14 NIV).

Jesus reassured John, telling him it was important to meet all of God's requirements, and John agreed to perform the rite. Jesus entered the Jordan River and was baptized by John.

As Jesus was baptized, he and John literally saw heaven open as the Holy Spirit descended in the form of a dove. As the dove hovered over Jesus, an audible voice from heaven spoke, saying, "This is my Son, whom I love, and I am very pleased with Him" (Matthew 3:17 NIV).

Then John said, "I saw the Spirit come down from heaven in the form of a dove and rest on Him. Until then I did not know who the Christ was. But the God who sent me to baptize with water told me, 'You will see the Spirit come down and rest on a man; He is the One who will be baptized with the Holy Spirit'" (John 1:32–34 NIV).

John the Baptist knew the prophecy, and from that moment on, openly declared and proclaimed that Jesus was the Messiah, the one and only Son of God.

John continued sharing the message God had given to him, spreading the news that the Messiah had come to earth to save all who would believe in Him. Even to his imprisonment and ultimate beheading, John proclaimed the good news to anyone who would listen, fulfilling God's plan for his life.

XXVI

Baptism, Temptations, Teaching, and Preaching

This is He who was spoken of through the prophet Isaiah: "A voice of one, calling in the wilderness, 'Prepare the way for the Lord, make straight paths for him'" (Matthew 3:3 NIV).

After John the Baptist shared these words, preparing the way for Jesus and his subsequent teaching, he baptized Jesus. Spreading the gospel of Jesus Christ and teaching others that Christ would baptize with the Holy Spirit, John tirelessly continued the work he was destined for—that of telling others "after me comes one who is more powerful than I, whose sandals I am not worthy to carry..." (Matthew 3:11 NIV).

Jesus began a forty-day fast and was led by the Spirit into the wilderness, where He was tempted by the devil three different times: to turn the stones of the wilderness to bread, to jump off the highest point (expecting angels to catch Him), and lastly to bow down and worship Satan. Each time, Jesus rebuked Satan with scripture, and finally the devil left Him.

God sent angels to attend to Jesus during His forty-day stay in the wilderness. He completed His fast, and upon hearing that John had been imprisoned, He left the wilderness for Galilee.

Recognizing His need to spread the word of the living God, Jesus began calling His disciples and once gathered spent three years teaching them. As disciples, He named Simon, called Peter; his brother, Andrew; James; John; Philip; Bartholomew; Matthew; Thomas; James, son of Alphaeus; Simon, called the Zealot; Judas, son of James, and Judas Iscariot.

As a crowd trailed behind Jesus, they were eager to hear His message. He traveled the countryside, and some immediately believed His message and followed Him.

Others, like Andrew and Peter, former disciples of John the Baptist, were invited to join Jesus in His ministry. Philip was approached directly by Jesus, saying "Follow me," and then Philip approached his friend Bartholomew. Though skeptical of this man from Nazareth, Bartholomew quickly changed his mind upon meeting Jesus, joining the group.

Similarly, Jesus issued a personal invitation to Matthew, a tax collector, who he found sitting at his tax booth. Jesus said to him, "Follow me," and Matthew immediately left his possessions behind and started following Jesus.

Before formally identifying His disciples, Jesus spent an entire night praying for guidance. In the morning He called together His large group of followers, and from them selected the twelve. From that day forward, and over the course of the next three years, the disciples would live with and learn from Jesus.

Jesus and His disciples traveled from town to town teaching the people. Always emphasizing compassion for others, He stressed the importance of devotion to the Lord.

Jesus's relationship with His disciples adhered to Jewish traditions. Jesus was the scholar who knew how to live to please God. Any disciple was expected to submit to His authority. Living and studying together, Jesus and the disciples He had chosen discussed every aspect of their daily lives.

Having several in His midst who were fishermen by trade, Jesus told them that He would make them "fishers of men." As they learned and grew in the knowledge Jesus imparted, they indeed became representatives of the good news that the Savior came to give all the people of the earth.

Then the disciples came and asked him, "Why do you speak to them in parables?" He answered, "To you it has been given to know the secrets of the kingdom of heaven, but to them it has not been given (Matthew 13:10–11 NIV).

Jennifer Taylor Wojcik
Philip G. Lilly D.Min.

The disciples were appropriately subservient to Jesus but, because they were fully human, lost their way from time to time. Such was the case when Jesus taught the crowds of people by using parables. These stories were simple in their form but profound in meaning. He had to remind the disciples of their ongoing teaching and the ability to relate the story in such a way that anyone could understand and grasp.

The Sermon on the Mount was Jesus's first address to the masses, and there He taught by His own methods. So the people would understand, He used a clear method of teaching, just as the rabbis had done with their students. Jesus taught with *authority*, leaving virtually no one to doubt His words.

On the Sunday morning before Passover, Jesus sent two disciples into the village of Jerusalem to find a donkey and her colt and instructed them to bring them back to Him. Jesus *told* the disciples they would be asked who the donkey was for and told them to say, "The Lord needs it." Perhaps those disciples recognized Jesus's *foreknowledge* of what would occur; perhaps they did not.

Why enter Jerusalem on the back of a donkey? To make a triumphal entry into the city, normally afforded to rulers and generals, Jesus declared that He came to the city as a ruler—the rightful heir to David's throne. This act fulfilled Zechariah's prophecy that the Messiah would enter Jerusalem on a colt. The disciples put robes on the colt, and Jesus mounted it and then headed into Jerusalem. Seen by the Passover crowds, they joined the procession, throwing their garments at the feet of the donkey and waving palm branches.

Perhaps some of the disciples realized what they had witnessed—perhaps not, but Jesus had just shown them His advance knowledge of *things to come.*

As Jesus continued to work with His disciples, He demonstrated many great works—from healing the sick and affirmed to practical life lessons about how to love your enemies, the consequence of sin, the needlessness of worry, and judging others. He taught them how to pray to the Father, and when the time was right, He gave them the authority to heal.

On three separate occasions, Jesus predicted His own death—each time sharing it as a warning to the disciples to be prepared. Each time Jesus spoke of His death, He also spoke of His resurrection.

At the Seder dinner—more commonly called The Last Supper—Jesus's concern was for his disciples. He used this final meal to prepare them for what was about to occur. After washing the feet of the disciples, He announced His upcoming betrayal by one disciple, denial by another, and abandonment by all of them when He was in danger. In every instance, the disciples refused to believe these things could happen.

> *"This is my body, which is given for you. Do this in remembrance of me...This cup that is poured out for you is the new covenant in my blood"* (Luke 22:19–20 NIV).

Breaking the bread as the body of Christ and blessing the wine as His blood, He gave thanks and handed a bit of each to every disciple. From this act, the Eucharist sacrament followed by most Christian denominations was instituted.

The disciples followed Jesus from the Upper Room where the Last Supper had occurred to the Garden of Gethsemane, where most of the twelve fell asleep. As Jesus walked deeper into the garden, He was accompanied by Peter, James, and John and asked them to keep watch—to stay awake and pray.

Anguished and now alone, Jesus threw himself to the ground, and three times asked His Father to spare His life.

Luke tells us in Chapter 22:44 that His pain was so great that "His sweat became like great drops of blood falling down on the ground," yet with each prayer Jesus concluded with "not what I want, but what you want, Father." Accepting that His father's will was for Him to die for the sins of the world, He acknowledged His fate and returned to His disciples.

Finding them sleeping, Jesus awaited His betrayal and arrest. Just as He had foretold, Judas Iscariot sold Him out for thirty pieces of silver, Peter denied knowing Him three times, and the disciples scurried away from Him as He was led away by the soldiers.

XXVII

The Anointed One

Happy are those who respect the Lord and obey him. You will enjoy what you work for, and you will be blessed with good things. Your wife will give you many children like a vine that produces much fruit. Your children will bring you much good, like olive branches that produce many olives. This is how the man who respects the Lord will be blessed (Psalm 128:1–4 NIV).

Iri had been blessed. His father's crop he'd inherited had provided anointing oil to prophets, priests, and kings because they were consecrated for the service of God. A person who received anointing oil was to be obeyed: the prophet as he spoke to the people *from* God; the priest who represented the people *before* God; and the king who established God's law.

Olive growing had long been a vital element of the food supply. Growing adjacent to Iri's house, the small trees he originally grafted from his grandfather's stock had become fruitful and multiplied. He now owned several olive groves that were planted near wine vineyards and grain fields, and his crop was bountiful. It had been more than fifteen years of growing time for most of his fields, and they had matured naturally with the guarantee that they would provide fruit for years.

Could it be that Jesus of Nazareth, a mere carpenter by trade, was the One prophesied about? Could this gentle man, who as a young lad had helped Iri when his olive cart was mired in a muddy stream, be the Chosen One?

When Iri heard the news that Jesus Christ—whom he had encountered twice before—was the Son of God, he could not wait to seek Him out.

Iri would fulfill his dream of providing anointing oil to the prophesied king. Iri's life had been filled with blessings, but having met the son of God? This was the blessing of all blessings! Iri vowed he would find Jesus as He traveled about the land, sharing the Christian message. He would once again meet Jesus of Nazareth and present Him with his very best oil.

"Crucify him!" they shouted (Mark 14:13 NIV).

Iri traveled as quickly as possible but reaching Jerusalem found the streets strangely vacant. When he inquired where everyone was, he was told about the punishment of sinners at Golgotha. Soon, news filtered down to Iri that Christ Jesus was to be crucified, as He had been found guilty under the Law and labeled the King of the Jews.

A large number of people followed Him (Jesus) including women who mourned and wailed for Him (Luke 12:27 NIV).

Iri arrived in Jerusalem and quickly made his way to Golgotha. He fought his way through the crowd, only to arrive at the crucifixion site where his friend, his Lord and Savior, was nailed to a cross between two common thieves.

There Iri approached two Roman soldiers, asking that he be allowed to anoint Jesus with oil. Scoffing at his request, the soldiers pushed him to the ground and told him to save his oil for a *real king.*

As he looked up from the ground where he lay, he squarely saw the face of Jesus, and he could not help but see that Jesus had recognized him. Iri uttered a prayer asking that God save him—and his family—and to please grant him pardon for being so late.

A peace came over Iri that he could not explain or ignore. He stayed there at the foot of Jesus's cross and did not leave until Jesus gasped His last breath on the cross.

The skies darkened, thunder rolled, and the earth seemed to shake on its axis. But Iri was not fearful—he was convinced that his friend, his Lord, had saved him. When the darkness ceased, Jesus's body was lowered to the ground. It was then that Iri ran to Him, took out his best anointing oil, and with it bathed the face of Jesus.

Joseph of Arimethea approached the Roman soldiers, stating that he had approval from Pilot to take the body of Jesus for burial. As the soldiers backed away, Joseph and Iri hurriedly attended to Jesus, as they had realized that the Sabbath was about to begin.

XXVIII

From the Cross—through his Eyes

"Now my soul is troubled, and what shall I say, 'Father, save me from this hour'?
No, it was for this very reason I came to this hour. Father, glorify your name!"
Then a voice came from heaven, "I have glorified it, and will glorify it again"
(John 12:27–28 NIV).

Alone—nailed to a wooden cross—He viewed those who stood at the foot of the cross before his death. There from His left to His right stood Lazarus, along with his two sisters, Mary and Martha; Iri, with the jar of anointing olive oil; Joseph of Arimethea, a disciple of Jesus, owner of the tomb in which Christ would be buried and holding the cloak Jesus would be buried in; John, his friend and apostle, alongside his mother, Mary; his mother's sister, Mary, wife of Clopas; his brothers and sisters and their spouses; and his friend, Mary Magdalene.

Lastly, he saw Saul of Tarsus, standing on the sidelines just as he had done when Stephen was stoned to death.

Among the crowd were some "disciples" of Christ—hooded and hidden in the shadows—those who dared not be recognized but were surely there. Among those was Peter, who had denied knowing Jesus three times, just as Jesus had said he would do.

Jesus looked to His mother Mary saying, "Dear woman, here is your son." Then to John, Jesus said, "Here is your mother." From then on John took Mary to live in his home" (John 19:26–27 NIV).

He saw those faces who mourned his vile treatment. He saw those who mocked him and chanted slurs and jeers as they passed by his cross. And he saw the Roman guards who showed no empathy for a man falsely accused yet condemned, just as the common criminals that hung on either side of him. There, in the midst of the Roman guards stood Pamphillius, the soldier who had once asked Jesus to bless him, and He had, standing on the docks of Charax.

The disciple John then moved up behind Jesus's mother, Mary, and placed his hands on her shoulders. Sensing who touched her, she reached up, grabbed onto him, and buried her face in his chest to cover her tears.

The soldiers made fun of Him, coming to Jesus and offering him vinegar to drink. They said, "If you are the king of the Jews, save yourself!" (Luke 23:37 NIV).

While the torture of Christ occurred, the crowd ebbed and flowed. Concealing their identities and camouflaged among those milling about were Mark, Luke, and Matthew—all devout followers of Jesus. As they separately wandered through the throngs of people, they all took note of what they saw and heard at the crucifixion. Those mental notes and images were translated into word accounts in the New Testament books authored by them. John also provided his account of that day's events in his gospel.

One can only imagine what these disciples witnessed and overheard, all the while maintaining their veiled appearance. John, standing alongside Jesus's mother, must have exercised great restraint in penning the grieving mother's reaction to all that happened in her presence.

Each apostle would have overheard a different group of bystanders—their jeers and insults or their grief for the dying Jesus. And while the accounts are eerily similar as reported in the gospels, each man had a different perspective.

Luke must have overheard the robbers who hung beside Jesus. As he reports, Jesus, in looking to either side, saw one thief to the left and a rebel and robber to His right. As the executioners had done, the robber scoffed at Him, saying, "Aren't you the Christ? Then save yourself and us" (Luke 23:39 NIV).

But the other criminal stopped the man's jeers by saying, "You should fear God! You are getting the same punishment He is. We are punished justly, getting what we deserve for what we did. But this man has done nothing wrong." Then turning to Jesus, he said, "Jesus, remember me when you come into your kingdom." And Jesus answered by saying,: "I tell you the truth, today you will be with me in paradise" (Luke 23:40–43 NIV).

Luke's account of this most intimate conversation was surely burned into memory as some of the last words ever spoken by Jesus. He may have heard Jesus sharing the good news of salvation with the robber who was jeering at Him along with the crowd. If so, how saddened Luke must have been to see this sinner hold onto his unbelief—in the face of the Savior—even to death.

In an effort to hasten the death of the thieves, the Roman guards broke their legs. As the guards lifted their clubs, the unruly crowd was hushed, knowing

Jennifer Taylor Wojcik
Philip G. Lilly D.Min.

full well what was coming. With the first blow struck to the thief on Jesus's left, a cacophony of groans could be heard from the spectators.

When they approached Jesus, he was already dead. So, as a last insult, they pierced his side with a spear. This fulfilled the prophecy of the Old Testament: "Not one bone will be broken..." (Psalm 34:20 NIV), and "They will look at the one they stabbed..." (Zechariah 12:10 NIV).

At the precise moment Christ died, a Levite priest was sitting just outside the Holy of Holies. He heard a loud ripping noise and turned toward the chamber curtain, where he watched the four-inch-thick drape inexplicably tearing from *the bottom up to the top*, symbolizing the separation of God and Man.

When Jesus died, darkness covered the sun. Earthquakes occurred, and all knew then, without question, that this *was* the Son of God.

As Christ's eyes closed in death, the light of the world grew dim. Yet, He saw the faces of *every* person who *was alive, had been alive*, or *would ever be alive*. It was for each of them—and each of us—that Jesus Christ died. He served Himself up as the blood sacrifice for you, me, her, him, and them. He paid the ultimate price to prevent us from hell and damnation throughout eternity.

This is Jesus Christ of Nazareth—scourged and publicly humiliated as "King of the Jews"—whose clothing was torn from him and divided up by soldiers who cast lots for it and whose worn sandals were stolen by an angry mob and likely tossed into the streets of Jerusalem.

This man—*God*—whose prayer was, "Father, forgive them, for they know not what they do."

XXIX

The Appointed Time

And Saul, yet breathing out threatening and slaughter against the disciples of the Lord went unto the high priest, and desired of him letters to Damascus to the synagogues, that if he found any of this way, whether they were men or women, he might bring them bound unto Jerusalem. And as he journeyed, he came near Damascus; and suddenly there shined round about him a light from heaven... (Acts 9:1–3 KJV).

Stephen, a deacon in the new church, had been in Jerusalem distributing food and aid to Christianity's poorer members while counseling forgiveness of sins through Jesus. A skillful orator of his beliefs—many of which contradicted Judaism—offended some members of the local synagogues.

One of those groups located and hired false witnesses to lie about Stephen's teachings, forcing Stephen to defend himself before a council of Jewish elders.

Saul was standing in the midst of that group in Jerusalem who were waiting for Stephen's speech to end. As he ended his defense, he raised his eyes to heaven and claimed to see Jesus standing at the right hand of God. Onlookers in the court became so angry they surrounded the deacon and stoned him to death.

Saul was there, holding the cloaks and coats of those who were belittling and stoning Stephen for his belief in Christ Jesus. The Pharisee was a devout Jew living in Jerusalem at the time. Well known for defending Judaism at all costs, Saul searched out and persecuted Jews who followed Christ on the grounds that they were blasphemers who should be punished.

Jennifer Taylor Wojcik
Philip G. Lilly D.Min.

Saul embarked on a mission to halt the further spread of Christianity and asked a priest for letters to the synagogues in Damascus. Setting off for Damascus—a distance of one hundred fifty miles from Jerusalem—he traveled, letters in tow, to arrest believers of Christianity and force them back to Jerusalem to face trial and punishment.

As Saul neared Damascus, a bright light appeared, shining around him, and he fell to the ground, blinded. He then heard the voice of Christ Jesus asking why Saul was intently persecuting Him and His followers. When Saul responded, he asked the speaker to identify himself. He then heard these words: "I am Jesus, whom you are persecuting. Get up now and go into the city. Someone there will tell you what you must do" (Acts 9:5–6 NIV).

When Saul heard that it was the voice of Jesus, he braced himself for the worst. All he could hope for now was a quick death. In the blink of an eye, Saul was totally blind. He reached for his eyes but could not remove the thickening scales that grew there. Ending up bewildered and confused, Saul was taken to a stranger's bedroom. Being left there for three days with thick scales on his eyes and no food or water, Saul could only look *inward*. He saw himself for what he was—a sinner—once blinded to the truth.

Alone in the room with his sins gripping his mind, he asked to be forgiven—to be redeemed. Ananias, a disciple of Jesus, came to Saul as directed by Christ, and returned his sight by the laying on of hands. As soon as Ananias touched the eyes of the Pharisee, he blessed him in the name of Jesus, and once again Saul's sight returned. Subsequently Saul was baptized and became known as Paul, one who was saved by grace and who had experienced a profound change.

Within a matter of days, Paul was proclaiming in synagogues that Jesus was the Christ, the Messiah, the true Son of God.

From that day on, Paul preached about Jesus with the same fervor he once used persecuting Christians. Going forth, Paul was doubted, plotted against, and threatened with death, but his faith remained steadfast.

As one of the most prolific writers of the New Testament, Paul no doubt recollected and cherished his encounters with Jesus of Nazareth.

Paul was no longer confused about the *appointed time*, or the *good news* Jesus had spoken of. This *was* the good news, and Paul now "got it."

XXX

In his Footsteps: Wearing the Master's Sandals

I want you to know, brothers and sisters that the gospel I preached is not of human origin. I did not receive it from any man, nor was I taught it; rather, I received it by revelation from Jesus Christ (Galatians 1:11 NIV).

Paul—as Saul—had achieved great status in the Jewish communities, following the Law of his forefathers and connecting his ancestry to the Jewish elite, a "Hebrew of Hebrews" (Philippians 3:5), and based on the Law, faultless.

After his conversion on the road to Damascus, Paul became one of the most powerful apostles who ever lived. His writings make up a large part of the New Testament, with points that range from intricate theology to his passionate letters to churches that were starting and, more often than not, struggling to exist.

Paul went from extolling his own virtues and achievements to sacrificing his own wellbeing to spread the word of Christ Jesus. He no longer bragged of his own life's work for his own sake but rather used his past as a *reason* to see a new future—one centered on faith in God. And by doing so, Paul helped to establish and unify a growing number of Christ-centered churches.

After the resurrection of Jesus and Paul's transforming meeting with Him on the road to Damascus, Paul had an opportunity to visit with Lazarus and his sisters, Mary and Martha.

Jennifer Taylor Wojcik
Philip G. Lilly D.Min.

As the four of them talked of their faith, Paul asserted that to his dying day he would share the good news of Jesus Christ to anyone and everyone who would listen.

Paul shared his newly created plans to visit towns and villages and establish meeting places where believers could safely gather and worship. He vowed to make the message of Christ his life's work.

Martha whispered in Lazarus's ear, getting a nod from her brother, and then excused herself from the room. She returned within minutes, carrying a much-worn yet still sturdy pair of sandals. Mary, who had washed the feet of Jesus with expensive perfume, gasped at the very sight of her sister carrying those sandals into the room.

Martha said, "Paul, we know all too well about doubt. When our brother died, we told Jesus that had He been here, Lazarus would be alive. Jesus brought him back to life after he had been dead for three days. At that time we were thankful, amazed, and ashamed of our doubtful nature. You too have had your disbeliefs, your doubts, but your eyes were opened by the Master. And now as you begin your journey to spread the word of our Lord and Savior, we believe it is only fitting that you should have a pair of the Master's sandals as you walk in His footsteps."

Martha placed in Paul's hands the worn sandals that had once been bound to the precious feet of Jesus. These were the same sandals that Martha's sister, Mary, had removed as she anointed Jesus's feet with sweet perfume.

Through tears Paul said, "I am moved at your generosity, but I am not worthy of the sandals of my Lord. It would be improper for me to tie them to my sinful feet."

Lazarus said, "Jesus would have wanted you to have them, and so do we. Take them—wear them, or simply carry them close to your heart."

But whatever were gains to me I now consider loss for the sake of Christ...I consider them garbage, that I may gain Christ and be found in him, not having a righteousness of my own that comes from the law, but that which is through faith in Christ—the righteousness that comes from God on the basis of faith (Philippians 3:7 NIV).

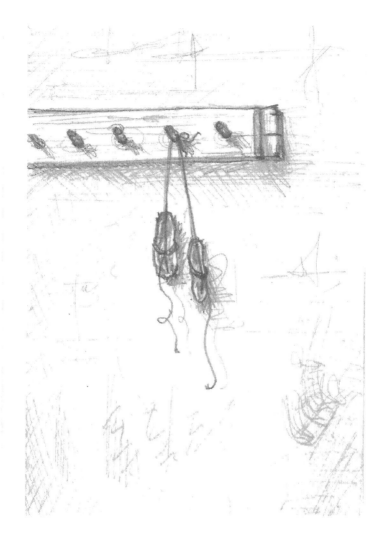

Footnote on Mary Magdalene

As Jesus predicted, He had traveled about from one town or village to another, sharing the good news of the kingdom of God. As He traveled, He was accompanied by the twelve disciples and also some women who had been cured of evil spirits or diseases. Mary Magdalene was one of those women.

The women assumed many tasks, including cooking, sewing, and laundry. Additionally, there was always the need for financial support to fund their sojourns, and Mary Magdalene was financially able to support these efforts.

She knew she could confide in Jesus and trusted His counsel from day one. He knew her flaws, and rather than reject her, He helped her deal with them. She was no doubt devoted to her new friend, as their subsequent encounters proved.

Once His powers of healing were fully developed, Jesus freed Mary Magdalene of her demons. Beyond that, we find Mary Magdalene at the mockery trial of Jesus as a witness to His sentence to die on the cross and standing next to His mother, Mary, at Golgotha. She assisted in His burial, and three days later was the first female to see the risen Christ.

Mary Magdalene became a friend to Jesus, seeing something in Him that fascinated her. Without realizing it at the time, she had found a friend for life.

A million stories have been told and/or written about Mary Magdalene. But one point is not disputable: she was a pivotal character in the life of Jesus and appeared several times in his life. While much has been *presumed* about her, she was a believer, friend, follower, and financial supporter of Jesus Christ and His ministry.

Epilogue

BEFORE THERE WAS TIME:
THE OTHER MISSING YEARS

Many of the missing years of Jesus happened before time (as we know it) began. He was there—a member of the divine Trinity—Father, Son, Holy Spirit—before the earth was formed and before time was recorded. We cannot fathom those years—or eons—because they cannot be quantified.

With but one decision made by *Him*, time and history began.

In the beginning God ("Elohim," which is plural) *created the heaven and the earth*...(explanation added, Genesis 1:1 NIV, KJV).

First this: God created the Heavens and Earth—all you see, all you don't see. Earth was a soup of nothingness, a bottomless emptiness, an inky blackness (Genesis 1:1–2 MSG).

In the beginning was the Word, and the Word was with God, and the Word was God. He was with God in the beginning. Through him all things were made; without him nothing was made that has been made. In him was life, and that life was the light of all mankind. The light shines in the darkness, and the darkness has not overcome it (John 1:1–5 NIV).

Jesus is the son of God, *and* He is fully God. He was sent by God to live a man's life on earth, albeit without the sin every other man has, as a gift to those who would believe. He supplied the blood sacrifice for *all*—for *every* sin.

Jennifer Taylor Wojcik
Philip G. Lilly D.Min.

For there is one God, and one mediator between God and men, the man Christ Jesus; who gave himself a ransom for all, to be testified in due time (1 Timothy 2:5–6 KJV).

From the manger to the cross, Jesus walked. Across deserts, mountains, valleys, and streams, he traversed all topography known to man. He experienced life. He experienced loss. He traveled the world to get to *know* the world in order to leave it a better place. He taught, loved, healed, and took the high road, always. He did all that He did for you and for me.

Now that you have taken this walk through the life of Jesus, your sandals are worn as well. Share His love, strap on His sandals, and carry with you the good news of Christ Jesus. May God richly bless and keep you.

Character Names

EXHIBIT I
Origin and Meaning

CHISION	ISRAEL	"HOPE/TRUST"
NATHAN	HEBREW	"GIFT/GOD GIVES"
RACHAEL	HEBREW	"SHEEPS FRIEND'
HIRAM	PHOENICIAN	"MY BROTHER LIFTED UP"
ELEORA	ISRAEL	"GOD IS LIGHT"
IRI	ISRAEL	"FIRE LIGHT"
JAYSON	GREEK	"HEALER"
MOSHE	HEBREW	"DRAWN OUT"
RUTH	HEBREW	"MATE/COMPANION"
ELYMAS	HEBREW	"ONE WITH INSIGHT"
AMIRA	HEBREW	"KING"
DERACH	HEBREW	"RICH"
TADEO	SPAIN	"PRAISE"
SAUL	HEBREW	"INQUIRED OF GOD"
HANNAH	HEBREW	"FAVOR/GRACE"
RHONDA	GREEK	"POWERFUL RIVER"
PAMPHILLIUS	ROMAN	"LOVES HORSES"

Family of Jesus of Nazareth

EXHIBIT II

Parents: Mary and Joseph
JESUS AT AGE TWENTY-FIVE

James—age twenty-three
Joses—age twenty-two
Judah—age twenty-one
Simon—age nineteen
Miriam—age seventeen
Assia—age sixteen
Lydia—age fifteen

Details/Definitions

EXHIBIT III

Adz—(pronounced *adds*); similar to an ax with an arched blade set at right angles to the handle

Archelaus—son of Herod, Ethnarch (4 BC– AD 6); the new ruler in Samaria and Judea

Arela —"angel" in Hebrew

Astron—(Greek) "the *given* star": believed to have *favored* the Jews

Bethlehem—"The House of Bread"

Cheder—(kheh'-der) bedroom

Denarii—Roman coins

Gifts from the Magi:
 Gold Coins;
 Frankincense—an aromatic resin that when burned produces a pleasant fragrance; and
 Myrrh—another gum or resin with a sweet aroma, used for making perfume, incense, and medicine

King Herod of Judea—(73 BC–AD 9)
Kislev—November

The Magi:
 Elymas ("one who has insight");
 Amira ("king"); and
 Derach ("rich")

Meshek—a light travel pack

Jennifer Taylor Wojcik
Philip G. Lilly D.Min.

Nebuchadnezzar II—king of Babylon (605–562 BC), conquered the southern kingdom of Judah in 586 BC

Regio Patalis—modern-day city of Thatta on the Hindus River

Soqet—watering trough for cattle

Yaqab—(Jacob) Joseph's father

Zechariah and Elizabeth—descendants of Aaron

Resources

Ahmad, Hadhrat Mirza. *Jesus in India*. Tilford Surrey: Islam International Publications LTD, 2003.

Barker, William. *Everyone in the Bible*. Westwood, New Jersey: Revell, 1966.

Bromiley, Geoffery W., ed. *The International Standard Bible Encyclopedia*, Grand Rapids: Eerdmans, 1979.

del Mastro, M.L. *All the Women of the Bible*, Edison, New Jersey: Castle Books, 2004.

Gardner, Joseph L., ed. *Atlas of the Bible*. Pleasantville, New York: Readers Digest Association, 1981.

Gower, Ralph. *The New Manners & Customs of Bible Times*. Oxford England: Moody Publishers, 2005.

Isbouts, Jean-Pierre. *Jesus: An Illustrated Life*. Washington, DC: National Geographic, 2015.

Rasmussen, Carl G. *Atlas of the Bible*. Grand Rapids: Zondervan, 2010.

Time-Life (Time Inc.), ed. *The Life of Jesus: How His Lessons, Miracles, and Devotion Changed the World*. New York: Time-Life, 2017.

Tyndale House Publishers, Inc., ed. *The Handbook of Bible Application: A Guide for Applying the Bible to Everyday Life*. Grand Rapids: Zondervan 2nd ed.

Vincent, Marvin R. *Word Studies in the New Testament*. Peabody, Massachusetts: Henrickson Publishers, 2009.

Made in the USA
Columbia, SC
23 February 2018